RELIGIOUS BELIEF AND RELIGIOUS SKEPTICISM

Religious Belief and Religious Skepticism

GARY GUTTING

UNIVERSITY OF NOTRE DAME PRESS
NOTRE DAME   LONDON

Copyright © 1982 by
University of Notre Dame Press
Notre Dame, Indiana 46556

Library of Congress Cataloging in Publication Data

Gutting, Gary.
    Religious belief and religious skepticism.

    Includes bibliographical references.
    1. Religion—Philosophy. 2. Belief and doubt.
I. Title.
BL51.G936   1982   200' .1   82-50287
ISBN 0-268-01613-5
ISBN 0-268-01618-6 (pbk.)

Manufactured in the United States of America

TO
MY MOTHER
AND
TO THE MEMORY OF
MY FATHER

Les doutes, in matière de religion, loin d'être des actes d'impiété, doivent être regardés comme des bonnes oeuvres, lorsqu'ils sont d'un homme qui reconnaît humblement son ignorance, et qu'ils naissent de la crainte de déplaire à Dieu par l'abus de la raison.

Diderot, *Addition aux Pensees Philosophiques,* I

Contents

Acknowledgments   xi

Introduction   1

PART I: The Need to Justify Religious Beliefs   11

1. The Wittgensteinian Approach   15

2. Aquinas on Religious Language   50

3. Disagreement and the Need for Justification   79

PART II: Justifying Religious Belief   109

4. Paradigms and Religious Beliefs   114

5. The Presence of God and the Justification of
   Religious Belief   141

Conclusion   178

Notes   181

Index   189

Acknowledgments

I want first of all to thank Fr. David Burrell, both for many stimulating and productive discussions over the years and for reading and commenting so helpfully on the whole of the book in manuscript. Stanley Hauerwas also read the entire manuscript and provided helpful comments. Others who offered valuable criticisms and suggestions include Dick Foley, Fred Freddoso, Tom Morris, Al Plantinga, and Ken Sayre. I am especially grateful to Karl Ameriks, whose careful and subtle comments on drafts of much of this book were very helpful.

Thanks are also due to Phil Devenish, with whom I have had many very helpful discussions of religion and to the members of my 1979 graduate seminar on religious belief, on whom I tried out early forms of many of the ideas in this book. A Notre Dame Faculty Development Summer Grant helped with the completion of the manuscript.

As always, my greatest debt is to my wife, Anastasia, for her never failing patience, encouragement, and love.

Introduction

Among the philosophical metadisciplines — e.g., philosophy of science, philosophy of history, political philosophy, aesthetics — philosophy of religion is peculiar in the suspicion with which it regards its subject matter. Think how odd it would be if the central question of the philosophy of science were whether science is at all worth pursuing, or if a major preoccupation of aesthetics were the propriety of writing poetry. And yet philosophy of religion, as practiced by believers and nonbelievers alike, has almost exclusively focused on whether there is any point to religious belief and practice.

This peculiar focus derives from the way philosophers of religion typically divide the world into believers and nonbelievers. Believers are presented as full of certainty about a most remarkable and, if true, utterly important set of claims. They accept wholeheartedly a detailed account of the ultimate origin, meaning, and destiny of our lives, and strive to act according to rules based on this account. Nonbelievers, in contrast, are persons of far more modest claims. They agree that it would be grand to share the believer's certainties about ultimate issues, but they just cannot see their way to an intellectually responsible endorse-

1

ment of so extraordinary a set of claims. Where the believer is committed, the nonbeliever abstains; and, because believers' claims are so strong, the question that naturally arises is why they maintain them. Given this way of opposing belief to nonbelief, philosophers of religion naturally find belief rather than nonbelief puzzling, and come to regard the object of their metadiscipline with suspicion.

I find this suspicion itself suspect. The nonbeliever set as a foil to the believer is portrayed in a thoroughly unrealistic way. Nonbelief in religion is in fact always the reverse side of some set of positive beliefs that regulate the nonbeliever's life. Not believing in God is just one aspect of believing in Marxism, liberalism, humanistic existentialism, materialism, or some other guiding set of secular beliefs. Even philosophers who like to think of themselves as skeptical critics of all presuppositions launch their critiques on the basis of substantial presuppositions about the privileged role of philosophical rationality (and, most often, one particular brand of philosophical rationality) as the guide of human life. In saying this, I am not trying to revive the disreputable ploy of claiming that we are all religious believers whether we realize it or not, nor am I suggesting that any evaluation of religious beliefs will beg the question. There is a division of great importance between those who hold religious beliefs and those who do not; and, as will appear, I think the conflicting claims of belief and nonbelief can be rationally adjudicated. My point is just that any disagreement between believers and nonbelievers involves substantial positive claims on both sides, so that the portrayal of nonbelief as mere withholding of assent is inaccurate.

The reason why nonbelief is not mere withholding of assent is that religion, throughout human history, has been an integral part of human life, attracting at all times the enthusiastic adherence of large numbers of good and intelligent people. To say that something that has such deep roots and that has been sustained for so long in such diverse contexts is nothing but credulity and hypocrisy is as extraordinary a claim as any made by religious believers. It may be true, but it can be legitimately asserted only on the basis of a well-developed and -supported nonreligious alternative. Further, since nonbelief (taken as a global questioning of the validity of religion) has such meager support in the history of the human race, at least the *initial* presumption of philosophy of religion should be in favor of belief rather than nonbelief. Here I am saying no more on behalf of religion than might be said, in the face of radical skeptical questioning, on behalf of science, art, morality, or any other pervasive achievement of human existence: that every presumption must be in favor of so central an element of our culture and that, lacking strong evidence for a contrary construal of human life, we should continue to assume its essential validity.

In proposing this revision in the orientation of philosophy of religion, I am not, however, attempting to insulate religion from philosophical criticism. My aim is to *refocus,* not eliminate, the project of a philosophical critique of religion. Because religion is a pervasive element of human culture and the source of some of its most splendid achievements, it would be very surprising to find that there is really nothing to it and that those who believe are just exhibiting their stupidity, credulity, or intellectual irresponsibility. But knowing that there is *some* essential truth to a view does not tell us what that truth is. Specifically, it does not follow that what there is to religion is what religious people and institutions have explicitly thought and said there is. Taking an enterprise as essentially sound is not the same as taking it at face value. We can both accept religion as somehow undeniably "right" and at the same time question severely the ideas that religions have of their own significance. In the same way, philosophers of science do not (and should not) take seriously the extreme skeptical suggestion that all claims of scientific knowledge are unwarranted. (They may rightly puzzle over how to meet the skeptical challenge, but this is a challenge to their philosophical accounts of science, not to science itself.) But this by no means implies that the philosopher of science accepts without question scientists' accounts of their enterprise and its significance. Jürgen Habermas, for example, accepts the validity of scientific knowledge and yet rejects unequivocally the positivist philosophy of science he attributes to many scientists as "scientistic self-misunderstanding." Similarly, even the most sympathetic philosopher of religion needs to be alert to "religious self-misunderstanding."

Religious self-misunderstanding can take two forms, corresponding to the content and to the manner of belief. First, even assuming that central religious claims are in some sense valid, it is entirely possible that a believer not understand them in this sense. To cite an example we shall discuss in some detail in chapter 1, D. Z. Phillips thinks that believers who regard prayer as a way of prevailing on God to intervene in our affairs have grossly misunderstood the true significance of this religious activity. Second, even if believers properly understand an article of their faith, they may assent to it in an inappropriate way. I shall particularly emphasize (in chapters 3 and 5) the dangers of giving "decisive" assent to claims that are worthy of only "interim" assent. (Roughly, decisive assent denies the epistemic need for further discussion of the claim assented to, whereas interim assent acknowledges such a need.) I shall argue that the self-misunderstanding of traditional religions is most apparent in their insistence on decisive assent to claims that are not worthy of such assent when given their traditional interpretations. The doctrines made most of by religions can be decisively assented to only if they are interpreted in ways that greatly dilute their traditional content.

The approach to philosophy of religion that I am suggesting is not prevalent. Contemporary philosophy of religion is, on the whole, a three-sided polemic among:

(1) those, such as Anthony Flew and Kai Nielsen, who see traditional religion as irrational superstition and offer philosophical arguments to show that it has no rational basis; (2) those, such as James Ross and Richard Swinburne, who think that traditional religious beliefs – at least the fundamental claim that God exists – can be established by rational argument; (3) those, such as Norman Malcolm and (to some extent) D. Z. Phillips, who maintain that the projects of philosophical criticism or defense of religious beliefs are fundamentally misguided because a religion is an autonomous framework not subject to external proof or refutation. Groups (1) and (3) obviously reject my construal of the philosophy of religion. Those in group (1) deny the assumption that religion has some essential validity; those in group (3) deny that there is room for philosophically based criticisms of religious beliefs. Those in group (2) are closest to my view: they accept the essential validity of religion and they allow that it is open to philosophical scrutiny. But they do not think that, in fact, philosophical problems about the justification of belief require any major modifications in the matter or manner of religious belief. By contrast, I shall argue that religious belief can be rationally justified, but the belief so justified is significantly different from the faith of most believers and their churches. In this way, my approach rejects the dichotomy between faith and skepticism on which most contemporary philosophy of religion is based. Religious belief is not something we must simply take or leave. Like science, art, and sexuality, religion is a human endeavor of undeniable significance and validity. The important philosophical question is not whether religion is true but rather what is the essential truth of religion and how does this truth fit with the de facto faith of believers.

The viewpoint I am proposing has very important consequences for the philosopher of religion concerned, as I am in this book, with the question of the justification of religious belief. Those interested in weighing the epistemic propriety of religious belief frequently take upon themselves the impressive burden of constructing (though often for imminent destruction at their own hands) elaborate philosophical arguments for the believer's fundamental assertions. Even if such constructions were successful, they would have no importance for the vast majority of believers, since in their elaborateness and subtlety, they are utterly implausible as explications of most believers' reasons for belief. My view, however, suggests that the philosopher of religion can look, with some expectation of success, at ordinary believers' actual, operative reasons for belief. If, as I presume, belief is not just credulity or irresponsibility, we should be able to find in the experience and thoughts of typical believers grounds that entitle them to their belief.

The idea that philosophically untutored believers have bases for their beliefs that have eluded highly sophisticated analyses may seem absurd, especially to philosophers who have firsthand awareness of the intricate problems encountered by, for example, even the apparently most straightforward arguments for theism. Nor is the absurdity entirely illusory. If we think that the traditional arguments for God's existence, as they are ordinarily construed, are paradigms of the way religious belief must be grounded, then it is obvious that hardly any believers are epistemically entitled to their faith. They simply do not have the resources for advancing even a fair approximation of a good argument of this sort. But there are other possibilities. The most prominent on the contemporary philosophical scene is the idea that believers' faith is so fundamental in their cognitive life that it is inappropriate (or, at least, unnecessary) to appeal to anything else to justify it. They are entitled to believe in God on the same grounds that they are entitled to believe in the external world, the reality of the past, and other minds: not because it is a conclusion for which they can give cogent reasons but because it is one of the basic beliefs by which their entire lives, including their projects of reason-giving, are regulated. Ordinary believers, it might be said, recognize this when they insist that their belief is simply a matter of faith and rightly ignore the irrelevant demands of skeptics that they prove what they believe. (Similarly, we are all rightly unintimidated by skeptical questions about how we know there is an external world, other minds, etc.) This view, especially as it has been developed by followers of Wittgenstein, is sensitive to some very important truths about religion, and I will devote part I of this book to a detailed examination of it. My conclusion, however, will be that the view is not ultimately defensible and that, accordingly, religious belief does require a justification.

The question, then, is what sort of justification is available, apart from something on the order of traditional arguments for God's existence. Here we need to reflect a bit on the sources of the failure of the traditional proofs as justifications of belief. The first source, already noted, is the dependence of one or more premises of such arguments on subtle and complex philosophical considerations that are beyond almost everyone. Believers cannot be secure in a faith based on an argument open to challenges they are incapable of meeting or even understanding. Another source is the fact that traditional arguments are what I call "one-dimensional"; that is, their cogency depends on the plausibility of each of the premises taken separately, so that if any one of the premises becomes questionable, the argument loses its force. Arguments of this sort are seldom appropriate supports of serious commitments in important matters. For, unless the argument's premises are extraordinarily uncontroversial, it is highly likely that those who rely on it will fairly soon have to face serious challenges to one of their essential premises. Indeed, belief will very likely have to be indefinitely suspended as challenge after challenge to one or another of the premises is met. Unless

the believer is eventually able to formulate a proof of hith-
erto unheard of obviousness, he or she will never be entitled to believe.

However, these failings of traditional proofs are not inevitable. There are, first of all, arguments (which I call
"multidimensional" rather than one-dimensional) in which
the premises overdetermine the conclusion; that is, the
conclusion is supported by a large number of different but
converging considerations and can remain cogent as a
whole even though some of the considerations (premises)
are questioned or rejected. Two arguments of this sort
seem to sustain the faith of very many religious persons.
One is based on the apparent power of a theistic framework to explain diverse features of our world and lives; the
other on the claim of many to have experienced the immediate presence of a divine being. Both arguments, as we
shall see, present cumulative cases for belief that do not
stand or fall with any one premise. They present belief as
legitimated not by a single chain of argument but by many
independent threads. Further, evaluating these arguments
does not require the resolution of any esoteric philosophical disputes, but only the sort of judgment that we all employ in countless everyday matters. Here we should expect
to find whatever justification there may be for religious belief. Part II is devoted to an examination of these arguments.

The argument from the overall explanatory power of
theism will turn out to be problematic. But, I shall argue,
the argument from religious experience does establish the
existence of a good and powerful being concerned about
us, and thus justifies a central core of religious belief. On
this basis, I shall argue that my assumption of the essential
validity of religion is vindicated and that accounts of reality
based on nonbelief are fundamentally inadequate. But I
shall also argue that the sort of religious belief I find justified falls far short of the claims of traditional religions and
that detailed religious accounts of reality are nearly as

suspect as nonreligious accounts. The heart of true religious belief is a realization that we can have *access* to God but only minimal reliable *accounts* of his nature and relations to us. This realization undermines the claims of both believers and nonbelievers who think they have essentially adequate pictures of the overall meaning and values of our lives. As a result, true religious faith is in fact a religious skepticism that deflates the pretensions of both belief and nonbelief.

PART I
The Need to Justify Religious Beliefs

There have always been disagreements about religion. But until what we call the modern age (i.e., the Enlightenment and after), the disagreements were about which religion to prefer, not, as today, whether belief in any religion at all is appropriate. We are still very far from understanding why this is so. The most popular explanations are based either on a naive faith in the intellectual perspicuity of the modern age, or on an equally naive cynicism about its unprecedented depravity. I will bracket the explanatory question and, simply taking the modern phenomenon of religious disagreement as a central fact, develop around it some reflections about the need for a justification of religious belief.

My primary topic in part I will be the idea, so popular in contemporary discussions of religion, that demands for a justification of religious beliefs are somehow inappropriate, that properly understood, believing is not something for which a person needs rational grounds. This is an initially surprising suggestion, given the fact of disagreement about religion. Ordinarily, disagreement about an important

11

matter among inquirers of apparently equal acuity and goodwill is taken to indicate that those who would take a position on the matter need to provide reasons for doing so. What no one has questioned I may, perhaps, take for granted; but where there is significant disagreement, it seems foolish simply to prefer my intuitions to those of others who seem to be my epistemic peers.

The most prominent suggestion has been that the case of religious disagreement is not an ordinary one, that there are features of religious beliefs and disagreements that make ordinary questions of justification irrelevant. My discussion in chapter 1 will focus on the development of this suggestion by Wittgenstein and his followers. The starting point will be Wittgenstein's musings, as recorded by his students, about the nature of religious disagreement. I begin by using his comments as a basis for constructing an account of the distinctive nature of religious disagreement. According to this account, religious disagreements are extraordinary in that there is an important sense in which the nonbeliever does not understand what the believer believes. However, I argue that this lack of understanding does not exclude the nonbeliever as a competent judge on religious matters. This eliminates one popular version of the view that religious beliefs need no justification: the one to that effect that only those who believe have an adequate understanding of what they believe. I next consider an even more important Wittgensteinian development of the no-justification theme: the idea that religious beliefs have a special epistemic role that makes demands for their justification inappropriate or even meaningless. Here I again begin with Wittgenstein's seminal remarks, but I also pay detailed attention to the ways his followers (especially Malcolm and Phillips) have developed them.

The conclusion of chapter 1 is that the Wittgensteinians have not made their case, primarily because they have not developed a detailed account of the nature of religious language to support the thesis that fundamental religious beliefs need no justification. It is, however, possible to evaluate the Wittgensteinian thesis on the basis of detailed accounts of religious language that are available from other sources. In chapter 2, I discuss one such account – Thomas Aquinas' as interpreted by David Burrell. This account seems particularly favorable to the Wittgensteinian thesis because it claims that we cannot properly make *any* statements about God but can speak of him only improperly (analogously) in a language uniquely applicable to him. I show, however, that even on this account the question of justification turns out to be appropriate and conclude that it is very doubtful that the Wittgensteinians can find any adequate account of religious language to support their thesis.

Finally, in chapter 3, I examine the suggestion that, even if the believer can neither justify his or her beliefs nor show that they have a special epistemic status that puts them in principle beyond justification, the believer is nonetheless entitled to them. I begin with Alvin Plantinga's recent claim that the believer may quite rightly take belief in God as an obvious example of a properly basic belief (i.e., a belief that needs no justification). As an obvious example of proper basicality, belief in God serves, for the believer, as a touchstone for criteria of proper basicality, and so needs no authenticating. I first argue that, since believers have "epistemic peers" who do not share their basic belief in God, there is nothing in their epistemic situation that supports the *truth* of this basic belief. So Plantinga's claim of proper basicality can at best mean that believers have a right to believe what they do quite apart from the question of the truth of their belief. Such a claim recalls the "principle of methodological conservatism" discussed in some recent epistemological work. According to this principle, those who believe a certain claim are entitled to continue believing it even though they come to see that there is no way of satisfactorily establishing its truth (providing they also see no satisfactory way of establishing its falsity). The last part of chapter 3 is concerned with attempts to formulate an acceptable principle of methodological conservatism and to apply it to religious belief. My conclusion is that, although an acceptable version of the principle can be formulated, its application to religion does not support the sort of assent that fundamental religious beliefs require. Accordingly, the overall conclusion of part 1 is that religious beliefs need no justification.

1. The Wittgensteinian Approach

1. Wittgenstein on Disagreement about Religion[1]

There is a standard model of disagreement in belief, applicable in many cases, that Wittgenstein thinks is irrelevant to religious belief properly construed. This is the *contradiction-model*: A says, "I believe in X" and B says either "I believe the opposite" or "There's no reason to believe such a thing." Here A and B are separated by B's denying or questioning what A affirms. Thus, someone says, "I believe in ESP" and another replies, "I believe in no such thing." Wittgenstein does not think this model applies to religious belief because, although he does not believe what the believer holds, he denies that he contradicts the believer's assertions:

> If some said: "Wittgenstein, do you believe in this?" I'd say: "No." "Do you contradict the man?" I'd say: "No."[2]

(Here "contradict" must be taken to include both denying an assertion and questioning it in the sense of saying there is no reason to believe it.)

I think Wittgenstein's line of thought here is roughly as follows: Suppose I find out that a friend, whom I have every reason to believe is as intelligent and reasonable as I, has a belief that I see as totally unwarranted (e.g., a belief that his illness is a punishment for his sins). Rather than

15

question my friend's rationality or intelligence, I am inclined to think that I do not properly understand what he
believes. When I do not understand someone's belief, I
neither share it nor contradict it.

But what is meant here by "understand"? As Wittgenstein says: "In one sense, I understand all he says — the
English words 'God,' 'separate,' etc." (*Lectures*, 55). This
thought is developed more fully in the following passage:

> The word 'God' is amongst the earliest learnt — pictures and
> catechisms, etc. But not with the same consequences as with
> pictures of aunts. I wasn't shown [that which the picture pic-
> tured]. . . .
>
> "Being shown all these things, did you understand what this
> word meant?" I'd say: "Yes and no. I did learn what it didn't
> mean. I made myself understand. I could answer questions, un-
> derstand questions when they were put in different ways — and
> in that sense could be said to understand" [p. 59].

Here Wittgenstein suggests a negative and a positive aspect
of his understanding of the word "God." Negatively, he
understands that the word does not refer to any of the ordinary objects accessible to our sense experience. God is
not like an aunt or any other far-distant, powerful, and
beneficent relative. This may not be immediately evident
to a child learning the word "God." After all, he may well
be taught to refer to persons whom he never sees but who
could be seen. Perhaps this is why Wittgenstein says "I
made myself understand." Of more importance for our
purposes is the positive sense in which Wittgenstein understands talk about God. He can answer questions about God,
even when they are put in different ways. But is this not
precisely to be able to play the religious language-game, to
know the rules for the use of the term "God," and hence
to understand its meaning? Wittgenstein grants this, but
insists that there is an important sense in which he still
does not understand.

What he has in mind is suggested by his comments about

what he would do if a friend claimed he was going to add numbers and proceeded to say "2 + 21 is 13" and other egregiously wrong things. Assuming that the friend was not joking or insane, Wittgenstein says, "In order to see what the explanation is I should have to see the sum, to see in what way it is done, what he makes follow from it, what are the different circumstances under which he does it, etc." (p. 62). A bit later he says: "What is the criterion for meaning something different? Not only what he takes as evidence for it, but also how he reacts, that he is in terror, etc." (p. 62). The idea in both these passages is that, besides understanding a statement by knowing how to use it, there is understanding it by knowing what sort of impact the statement has on the lives of those who believe it. Or, putting it another way, there is a sense of understanding what someone says for which it is necessary to see how the statement relates to the *nonlinguistic* dimensions of its user's life.

It seems to me that an excellent explication of what Wittgenstein means here is provided by Sellars' distinction between transitions *within* a language-game (i.e., transitions from one linguistic expression to another) and transitions that bring us into or take us out of the language-game (e.g., transitions from experiences to statements or from statements to actions).[3] The first sort of transition Sellars calls a *move* of the language-game. Moves are, in a broad sense, inferences (deductive or inductive, formal or material) from one assertion (position in the language-game) to another. Thus in English there is a legitimate move from "This wine is red" to "This wine has a color." Entry-transitions and departure-transitions are not moves: they do not take us from one position (assertion) in the language-game to another. Rather, they bring us to a position in the language-game from some extralinguistic "position" (e.g., a given stimulus of the sense organs) or they take us from a position in the language-game to some extralinguistic "position" (e.g., an action). The former is a *language-entry transition*; for example, my seeing a giraffe, followed by my saying (or thinking), "Here is a giraffe." The latter is a *language-departure transition*; for example, my saying, "That giraffe ought to be removed," followed by my removing it.

Returning to Wittgenstein's understanding of what his friend believes, the above distinctions suggest that he understands his friend's religious language-game in the sense that he is familiar with its moves and can even, at least to some extent, make them himself (as he would, e.g., if explaining Christianity to a Hindu). But this does not mean that he understands the language-game in the sense of knowing what sorts of experiences (observations, feelings, etc.) are appropriate antecedents to making a certain statement or which actions are the appropriate sequels to making certain statements. In short, it is possible to understand the moves of a language-game without understanding its entry- and departure-transitions. Or, to use a way of speaking employed in the *Lectures,* Wittgenstein may understand the "picture" his friend has — i.e., he sees how the different parts fit together in a coherent way — but he does not see how the picture "regulates" his friend's life.[4]

But could Wittgenstein not come to understand the entry- and departure-transitions of his friend's language-game? He could, but it would seem that to do so would be to become a believer. Entry- and departure-transition rules correlate nonlinguistic items (experiences or actions) with linguistic expressions.[5] Understanding a transition rule of course requires having the concepts in terms of which the rule characterizes the nonlinguistic items to which it refers. Further, having a concept requires an ability to recognize situations to which the concept is applicable. For example, an entry rule (of thumb) for the language of wine-tasting is, "If the wine has a strongly tannic taste, predict that it will have a long life." Clearly, if I do not have the concept of "having a strongly tannic taste," I cannot understand this rule. And, if I cannot, in at least some typical cases, recognize a strongly tannic taste, I do not have this concept. (When a concept is definable in terms of other concepts that I have, I may *infer* its applicability to a given situation even if I am not capable of directly recognizing this applicability. But having the basic undefined concepts of a language requires the ability of direct recognition.)

Now there are some cases in which the nonbeliever has the concepts involved in the transition rules of a religious language-game. Thus, believers may enter their religious language-game by praying when they feel stress. But in many centrally important cases, the concepts involved in a transition rule will have a specifically religious character. A feeling (antecedent to expressions of joy) may be characterized as "of God's special presence"; an experience (antecedent to prayers of thanksgiving) may be said to be "of God's providential assistance"; an action (following a reading of the Gospels) may be described as "treating another person as a child of God." It seems impossible for someone who does not believe to be able to recognize things as having these sorts of characteristics. A nonbeliever can of course recognize feelings of awe and mystery, experiences of being saved from imminent danger, and actions of unselfish kindness. But these are not experiences and actions as they are characterized in the rules of the religious language-game. Indeed, feelings of awe and mystery, and the like, may as such have no religious significance at all for the believer (e.g., a feeling of awe and mystery may result just from an encounter with an artist's genius). But if the nonbeliever is not able to recognize instances in which concepts such as 'being a feeling of God's presence,' 'express God's providential love,' and so forth, are applicable, the nonbeliever cannot be said to have these concepts.

To this conclusion there are two related objections. The first is that it is not a matter of nonbelievers' not being capable of recognizing instances in which religious concepts are applicable, but merely a matter of their belief that they have never encountered such instances. I have never recognized any animal that falls under the concept "living diplodocus" but I nonetheless have the concept of such an animal. However, in such cases I do have some implicit understanding of the rules relevant to classifying something as an instance of such a concept (e.g., a living diplodocus would have to be very long, capable of moving around, etc.). This leads to the second objection: Why could not the nonbeliever understand the believer by understanding the rules relevant to the recognition of items as characterized by religious concepts? Then the nonbeliever would understand the believer, and their disagreement would be about only the existence of items falling under these concepts.

The point of these objections is sound for cases in which the believer's application of religious concepts is simply a matter of *interpreting* certain occurrences (experiences, actions), shared by the believer and the nonbeliever, in religious terms. Thus, a child dies in agony and the believer says, "It was God's will." The believer did not have an experience of the child's death as being an expression of God's will. He had the same experience of the child's death that the nonbeliever had and imposed the categories of his religious language-game to interpret the event as being in accord with God's will. If the believer's application of religious concepts were always of this sort, then there would be no reason to say that nonbelievers cannot understand believers. But if religious views were nothing more than systems for the after-the-fact interpretations of experiences, then they would not have the capacity for eliciting the profound commitment typical of religious belief. There would be no avoiding the fact that this is just one way of looking at things. But as a matter of fact religious beliefs — at least those involving a deep personal commitment — are almost always sustained by experiences in which the world is directly encountered in religious terms. Believers do not feel awe and mystery (just as nonbelievers might) while staring at the starry sky above and then interpret this feeling as a manifestation of the divine presence. They simply have feelings of the divine presence (or of God's providential care for them, or of the Spirit's action in their community).

This is not to say that the believer's "religious experiences" are pure givens, with no interpretive element. Like all experiences they presuppose a certain conceptualization. It is just that this conceptualization is an intrinsic part of the experience, not an interpretation imposed after the fact. We need accordingly to distinguish two senses of "interpretation," the first (external interpretation) referring to a conceptualization imposed on an already given experience and the second (internal interpretation) referring to a conceptualization implicit in the experience itself. In the latter case we can say the concepts "constitute" (are essentially involved in) the experience. Nonbelievers do not understand believers, because they do not have access to the internal interpretations involved in the entry- and departure-transition rules of the religious language-game.

Of course it is true that there are rules corresponding to the believer's internal interpretation of religious experience. For the application of concepts, whether it is a matter of internal or external interpretation, is always (at least implicitly) a rule-governed procedure. Given this, it might be suggested that the nonbeliever can still understand the believer by understanding the rules of these internal interpretations. But this suggestion is based on a misunderstanding of the nature of experiences and the concepts involved in them. Consider the simple but typical case of our experiences of colored objects. These experiences involve internal interpretations via a system of interrelated concepts such as 'color,' 'shade,' 'tone,' 'appearance,' and 'lighting conditions.' The rules relevant to such experiences express various interconnections between these concepts; thus: "If an object looks green in ordinary light, say it is green." One can understand these rules only by first understanding the concepts in terms of which they are expressed. Someone who has no concept of color will not be able to get it by memorizing rules connecting this concept with others in the same system. The concept can be acquired only by undergoing a process of training (behavioral conditioning) that will result in an ability to make direct reports about the colors of various objects in various circumstances. The same is true of any concept constitutive of an experience, including specifically religious concepts. The concepts can be acquired only as part of the process of coming to have the experiences constituted by the concepts. This is not of course to say that the concepts are derived (e.g., abstracted) from experience. Rather, acquiring the concepts and coming to have experiences constituted by the concepts are part of the same epistemic process.

Our explication of Wittgenstein's point is, in summary, this: nonbelievers can understand believers in the sense of knowing how to make the intralinguistic moves of the religious language-game. But they cannot understand believers in the sense of possessing (all) the concepts that constitute believers' experiences of the world in specifically religious terms. They do not possess these concepts, because they have not had the characteristically religious experiences that are essentially tied to their acquisition.

Does it follow that nonbelievers are not competent judges of the truth of religious claims and that, accordingly, believers need not take disagreement as a serious challenge to belief? Such a conclusion would be too hasty. First, as we saw, Wittgenstein's nonbelievers do understand belief in the sense of knowing the *moves* of the religious language-game. Because of this they can at the very least raise questions about the internal consistency of a system of religious beliefs that must be satisfactorily answered by the believer. At least to this extent, their lack of understanding does not allow nonbelievers to ignore the believer's views. However, this point is askew of the issue at hand, which is whether, given a lack of compelling arguments for or against belief, the believer need be concerned about the negative (atheistic or agnostic) "intuitive" judgment of the nonbeliever about religion.

What advantage in understanding does the believer have over the nonbeliever? It consists in having certain concepts in the sense of being able to have experiences of objects as falling under these concepts. If the issue were whether or not there are religious experiences (experiences constituted by specifically religious concepts), then the believer's advantage would be decisive. But the issue is about the veridicality of these experiences, not their occurrence; and here the believer has no special competence as a judge. For the veridicality of an experience is not something that depends primarily on "phenomenological" features of the experience (e.g., its vividness, clarity, intensity, etc.) that are accessible only to those having the experience. Rather, veridicality depends primarily on the way the experience is related to other experiences, in particular the expectations induced by the experience (more precisely, the past and present experiences pointed to as likely occurrences, given the veridicality of the experience in question). Hence, being in a position to assess the veridicality of an experience requires only knowing that certain sorts of experiences have or have not occurred, not actually having any of the relevant experiences. Thus, the congenitally blind are entirely competent to judge the veridicality of color-experiences, provided they have reliable information about the sorts of experiences that have occurred. Similarly, theoretical chemists may rightly question the correctness of microscopic observations that they themselves are not capable of making. Indeed, we should sometimes discount the intuitive judgments of observers about the veridicality of their observations because of the natural desire to believe that one has seen truly. (Of course it is also often true that experiencers' believing that they have truly seen can count in favor of the veridicality of their experience — for example, if they are well trained and have a good record. The point is that in all cases the evidentiary force of experiencers' belief can be competently assessed by those who have not had the same experience.)

The point I am making can also be put as follows: supposing the veridicality of a given religious experience (e.g., of a good and powerful being concerned about my moral state), there are further experiences that we should anticipate (with probability if not certainty) because of the rules governing the *moves* of the religious language-game (e.g., experiences of aid in our efforts at moral improvement). Nonbelievers, as we have seen, are entirely capable of understanding these moves. Therefore, supposing (as we are) that they accept believers' reports of the occurrence of their various experiences, nonbelievers are accordingly able to make an informed judgment about the experiences' veridicality. To judge the veridicality of an experience, we need only understand the moves of the language-game that define the concepts constituting it. We do not need to understand the entry- and departure-transitions of this game. The believer may of course be right about the veridicality of religious experience. But if so, the belief needs to be based on a defense of the veridicality of the experience. (In chapter 5, I offer such a defense.)

In summary, then, the advantage in understanding that the believer has over the nonbeliever amounts to the fact that the believer is capable of having experiences not available to the nonbeliever. However, this difference, for all its importance, does not show that only the believer is in a position to evaluate religious claims. For the evaluation of these claims requires assessing the veridicality of these experiences, and the inability of nonbelievers to have the experiences does not make them incompetent at this assessment. So I conclude that the nonbeliever's lack of understanding does not support the conclusion that religious beliefs require no justification.

2. Wittgenstein on the Special Status of Religious Beliefs

Wittgenstein's musings about religion suggests another way of arguing that disagreement about religion does not require believers to offer justification of what they believe. This is the idea that religious beliefs fall outside the category defined by the reasonable/unreasonable distinction and so cannot be properly subjected to the process of justification (giving reasons). It is this idea, more than any other, that has influenced contemporary arguments for the irrelevance of justifications of religious beliefs.

Wittgenstein's thought here begins with certain cases of religious disagreement to which it would seem that the standard contradiction model does apply. For example, a Father O'Hara claimed that religious belief can be soundly based on scientific evidence. Wittgenstein says: "I would definitely call O'Hara unreasonable. I would say, if this is religious belief, then it's all superstition" (p. 59). Certainly, to respond to someone's "I believe in X" with "That's unreasonable, it's superstitious" is to contradict that person (in Wittgenstein's sense).

But Wittgenstein also makes it clear that he thinks there is something wrong with a believer who presents his or her belief in a way that occasions this sort of disagreement. Of O'Hara's "unreasonable" belief he says: "But I would ridicule it, not by saying it is based on insufficient evidence. I would say: Here is a man who is cheating himself" (p. 59). O'Hara then has fallen into a misunderstanding of his own belief (indeed, a "scientistic misunderstanding") that deprives him of its true significance. (So it seems that believers as well as nonbelievers can fail to understand belief!)

Why does Wittgenstein say O'Hara misunderstands his own belief? Why is it "ludicrous" for him to present religious beliefs as reasonable claims based on evidence? Because, at least in the ordinary sense, evidence has nothing to do with religious belief:

These controversies look quite different from any normal controversies. Reasons look entirely different from normal reasons.
They are, in a way, quite inconclusive.
The point is that if there were evidence, this would in fact
destroy the whole business.
Anything that I normally call evidence wouldn't in the slightest
influence me.
Suppose, for instance, we knew people who foresaw the future; made forecasts for years and years ahead; and they described
some sort of a Judgement Day. Queerly enough, even if there
were such a thing, and even if it were more convincing than I have
described . . . , belief in this happening wouldn't be at all a religious belief [p. 56].

Wittgenstein connects the irrelevance of evidence with the
nature of the commitment to religious belief. He notes, for
example: (1) the oddity of saying that believers hold the
opinion that there will be a Last Judgment ("dogma" or
"faith" are more appropriate expressions); (2) the special
sense of "believe" operative in religious contexts (ordinarily we would say, "You only believe – oh well . . ."
[p. 60]; but here the belief is "unshakable" [p. 54]); (3)
the great distance between the believer who says "There
will be a Last Judgment" and someone who says "Possibly,
I'm not so sure" in contrast to ordinary situations – for
example, a discussion about whether a tree is an elm –
where two people disagreeing in this way would not be regarded as far apart. Wittgenstein's point is not that the believer *feels* totally certain about a belief ("The strength of
a belief is not comparable with the intensity of a pain"
[p. 54]) but that the belief exercises an unconditional control over the believer's actions. The believer is like a person
fighting against being dragged into a fire: "No induction.
Terror" (p. 56). But we need to be careful of this striking
comparison. The point is not that religion is a matter of
emotion, rather than reason. Rather, the commitment of
the believer, like the struggle of the person trying to escape

the fire, has an unequivocal, unhedged quality that makes any appeal to evidence irrelevant. Accordingly, Wittgenstein wants to say that religious belief, properly understood, is neither reasonable nor unreasonable:

> ... Am I to say they are unreasonable? I wouldn't call them unreasonable.
>
> I would say, they are certainly not *reasonable*, that's obvious.
> 'Unreasonable' implies, with everyone, rebuke.
>
> I want to say: they don't treat this as a matter of reasonability.
>
> Anyone who reads the Epistles will find it said: not only that it is not reasonable, but that it is folly.
>
> Not only is it not reasonable, but it doesn't pretend to be.
>
> What seems to me ludicrous about O'Hara is his making it appear to be *reasonable* [p. 58].

The idea behind these comments is developed more clearly in Wittgenstein's reflections (especially in *On Certainty*) on the special role some beliefs play in our "form of life." For example, many actions I perform every day are based on the belief that I have two hands (e.g., my presently typing these words). It may seem that these actions are rational only if I have evidence for the claim that I have two hands. But Wittgenstein points out that it is foolish to speak, in an ordinary context, of my having evidence that I have two hands.[6] For anything I might put forward as evidence (observations, reports of others, etc.) would itself be more reliable than the belief that I have two hands. (We can imagine extraordinary cases where this would not be so – e.g., I wake up in a hospital after a bad accident with bandages up to my elbow.) The principle involved here is an important one, for it shows that what is going on when we ask what someone actually may or should believe cannot be entirely explicated via relations of confirmation between propositions. Account must also be taken of how a belief is placed in a given believer's "system" of beliefs. Some beliefs are – at least at a given time – so deeply

embedded that it is pointless to support them with anything else (e.g., "my not having been on the moon is as sure
a thing for me as any grounds I could give for it."[7]) This is
not to say that I cannot (inductively or deductively) derive
such a belief from others: ". . . any proposition can be
derived from other ones. But they may be no more certain
than it is itself."[8]

We may want to reserve the appellation "rational" for
actions that can be justified by citing the evidence for the
beliefs on which they are based; and we may wish to call a
belief rational only if we are entitled to it because of evidence. But then we must admit that there are cases where
actions and beliefs are appropriate even though they are
not rational. There will have to be cases of actions and
beliefs that are neither rational nor irrational but that are
also entirely "proper."

But is religious belief one of these cases? Wittgenstein,
as we saw, suggests that religious beliefs are so central in
the lives of those who hold them that there is nothing
more "certain" that could be put forward in evidence of
them. A major objection to this view — urged by many
critics — is that a belief can be utterly central for a believer
and be nonetheless entirely irrational. There are those who
are as certain as they are of anything that the earth is flat,
that sex is vile, that the CIA is stalking them; and we rightly
see their beliefs as foolish, fanatical, or neurotic. Centrality
may mean that a belief is psychologically (or, for deluded
groups, sociologically) fundamental but not epistemically
privileged. Why should we think this is not the case with
religion?

The answer presumably is that there is some other feature of religious beliefs that is sufficient to make the question of justification irrelevant to them. What might this
be? The only plausible answer seems to lie in the fact that
these beliefs are presupposed by the very project of justifying them. This idea is only hinted at in Wittgenstein's
Lectures; though prominent in *On Certainty*, it is seldom

explictly connected there to religious belief. However, other philosophers — particularly Norman Malcolm, Peter Winch, and D. Z. Phillips — have developed the connection in detail. We turn next to their ideas.

3. Wittgensteinians and the Special Status of Religious Beliefs

According to Malcolm, any question about the justification of a belief must be raised within a "system" that "provides the boundaries within which we ask questions, carry out investigations, and make judgments."[9] The boundaries imposed by a system are defined by its "framework principles" — propositions that are taken for granted by everyone carrying out justifications within the system.

Malcolm offers a number of examples of framework principles: the belief that "familiar objects do not cease to exist without some physical explanation" ("The Groundlessness of Belief," 143–44), that there is a continuity of nature, that calculations are sufficiently checked once certain procedures are carried out, that we live on the earth, and a variety of beliefs about our "inner states" (e.g., about what we were going to say when interrupted, about what our intentions are, that following a given rule means acting in a particular way). Given the role of framework principles in a system, there is no sense to demands to justify *them*:

> Hypotheses are put forth, and challenged, *within* a system. Verification, justification, the search for evidence, occur *within* a system. The framework propositions of the system are not put to the test, not backed up by evidence [p. 146].

It is crucial to be clear why framework principles are not supported, may not be supported, by evidence. On the one hand, this is not because they are "self-evident" or "self-justifying." Framework principles have no intrinsic necessity, and we have no insight into their truth. Indeed, Malcolm insists that there is nothing intrinsically incoherent or unreasonable in the rejection of a framework principle. We can well imagine societies based on framework principles contrary to ours, and we have no basis for saying that we would be right and they wrong. On the other hand, the fact that framework principles cannot be justified is not a contingent fact, due perhaps to human weakness before the task of such a justification. The existence of unjustified and unjustifiable beliefs ("groundless beliefs") is necessary for the existence of any procedures of justification at all. "It is a conceptual requirement that our inquiries and proofs stay within boundaries" (p. 146). This is because the very notion of justification involves the notion of an *end* to justification. As Wittgenstein says for the case of the justification of mathematical claims by calculation: "In certain circumstances . . . we regard a calculation as sufficiently checked. What gives us a right to do so? . . . Somewhere we must be finished with justification and then there remains the proposition that *this* is how we calculate" (*On Certainty*, par. 212; cited by Malcolm, p. 147). The proposition that *this* is how we calculate (or, more generally, justify) is precisely a framework proposition. Accordingly, although neither self-justifying nor justifiable by argument, framework principles are not arbitrary stipulations but have an authority rooted in the practice of the linguistic community that employs the system whose boundaries they define.

When a system is employed by a linguistic community to justify beliefs, the system and its framework principles are normative for the language-game of the community. Further, a language-game involves some procedures of justification and hence must be based on the acceptance of some framework principles. Once again, Malcolm cites Wittgenstein: ". . . a language-game is only possible if one trusts something" (*On Certainty,* par. 509).

Applying these considerations to religious belief requires

only the recognition that the basic tenets of a religious faith are framework principles for a religious language-game. This does not mean that there is no such thing as an unwarranted or false religious belief. Religious language-games involve standards of justification that can be and are used to discredit or support various views. In this, Malcolm contends, religion is entirely on a par with scientific systems of thought such as chemistry:

> Within each of these two systems of thought and action there is controversy and argument. Within each there are advances and recessions of insight into the secrets of nature or the spiritual condition of humankind and the demands of the Creator, Savior, Judge, Source. Within the framework of each system there is criticism, explanation, justification [p. 152].

So there is no suggestion that religious beliefs as such have some peculiar immunity from rational evaluation. The point is just that, as in any other case, the enterprise of justification must (logically) be based on framework propositions that are themselves *groundless* (i.e., inappropriate objects of the process of justification). Thus, the text cited above concludes: "But we should not expect that there might be some sort of rational justification of the framework itself." In particular, the justification of religious claims is possible only on the basis of the groundless acceptance of some basic religious claims (the framework principles of a religious language-game).

There are two main ways of attacking Malcolm's view. The first, with which I do not sympathize, would quarrel with the antifoundationalist claim that justification must stop with propositions not themselves self-evident or otherwise self-justifying. The difficulties of giving an account of knowledge as based on incorrigible foundations seem to me insurmountable; and if the alternative seems to be a skeptical denial of the possibility of knowledge, then we had better rethink our understanding of knowledge. The second line of attack accepts Malcom's general epistemological approach but objects to the way he applies it to the case of religion. Just because the very process of justification requires groundless beliefs and religion involves processes of justification, it does not follow that "God loves us," "Jesus is God," and other fundamental religious propositions are properly believed without grounds. For a particular mode of justification (embedded in a particular language-game) may itself require justification via more fundamental justificatory procedures. For example, we may be in the habit of justifying claims about tomorrow's weather by appealing to the authority of reports given on local radio stations; but this entire procedure of justification is open to and requires justification on the basis of — for example — inductive evidence for the reliability of the reports relied on. A framework principle in Malcolm's sense must not only provide a basis for a process of justification, it must also not itself fall within the scope of some more basic process of justification. In this sense, the "system" specified by a set of framework principles must be autonomous. The suggestion of many critics has been that this is not so for religious belief.[10]

The possibility the critics have in mind is one defenders of the Wittgensteinian approach to religion are well aware of. Consider for example the following comment by Peter Winch:

> Concepts of witchcraft and magic in our culture, at least since the advent of Christianity, have been parasitic on, and a perversion of other orthodox concepts, both religious and, increasingly, scientific. To take an obvious example, you could not understand what was involved in conducting a Black Mass, unless you were familiar with the conduct of a proper Mass and, therefore, with the whole complex of religious ideas from which the Mass draws its sense. Neither would you understand the relation between these without taking account of the fact that the Black practices are rejected as *irrational* (in the sense proper to religion) in the system of beliefs on which these practices are thus parasitic. Perhaps a similar relation holds between the contemporary practice of astrology

and astronomy and technology. It is impossible to keep a discussion of the rationality of Black Magic or of astrology within the bounds of concepts peculiar to them; they have an essential reference to something outside themselves. The position is like that which Socrates, in Plato's *Gorgias,* showed to be true of the Sophists' conception of rhetoric: namely, that it is parasitic on rational discourse in such a way that its irrational character can be shown in terms of this dependence.[11]

Winch is pointing out that the meaning of concepts involved in certain language-games may be related to the concepts of other language-games in such a way that the claims of the first game can be evaluated on the basis of the justificatory practices of the second game. He recognizes, therefore, a connection between the meaning of a statement and the sort of considerations appropriate for its evaluation. This connection is in fact crucial for his reply to Alasdair MacIntyre's claim that the beliefs of the Zande tribe about witchcraft are irrational. For Winch admits that if the Zande beliefs are taken as hypotheses about the causes of things (in our scientific sense of "cause"), then they are irrational. However, he insists that the standards of scientific justification are not appropriate, because Zande beliefs do not have a scientific meaning:

> MacIntyre believes that he is applying as it were a neutral concept of 'A affecting B', equally applicable to Zande magic and western science. In fact, however, he is applying the concept with which *he* is familiar, one which draws its significance from its use in scientific and technological contexts. There is no reason to think that the Zande magical concept of 'A affecting B' has anything like the same significance.[12]

The beliefs on which Zande magical rites are based are not scientific, because they are not meant as descriptions of the world that provide a basis for controlling its contingencies. Rather, they are a particular way of recognizing and coming to terms with these contingencies. A scientific hypothesis excludes certain contingencies; the Zande beliefs are meant to provide a way of understanding the world no matter what the contingencies.

The importance of Winch's discussion for our consideration of religious belief is this: It suggests that our evaluation of Malcolm's claim that fundamental religious beliefs are framework principles of an autonomous system of justification will depend on our view of the kind of meaning these beliefs have. On some construals of this meaning, religious beliefs may well be properly accepted as groundless; on others they may fall within the scope of other justificatory procedures.

D. Z. Phillips has been especially sensitive to this point. He emphasizes in particular that if religious beliefs are taken as empirical hypotheses about the course of contingent events, then they are irrational superstitions; and that the inappropriateness of demands for justification of fundamental religious beliefs is apparent only if we understand the unique sort of meaning they have. To see both the power of this approach and the difficulties it encounters, let us reflect on Phillips' discussion of two specific loci of Christian religious beliefs: the practice of petitionary prayer and the doctrine of immortality.

Phillips thinks that there are common ways of interpreting petitionary prayer that do make it a superstitious practice:

> A boxer crosses himself before the fight — a mother places a garland on a statue of the Virgin Mary — parents pray for their child lost in a wreck. . . . Does the boxer think that anyone who crosses himself before a fight will not come to serious harm in it? Does the mother think the garland's value is prudential? Do the parents believe that all true prayers for the recovery of children lead to that recovery? If these questions are answered in the affirmative, the beliefs involved become testable hypotheses. They are, as a matter of fact, blunders, mistakes, regarding causal connections of a kind. We can say that the people involved are reasoning wrongly, meaning by this that they contradict what we already know. . . . But perhaps the activities have a different meaning.[13]

What sort of "different meaning" might be involved? Phillips suggests that the actions may not be attempts to influence God to act one way rather than another but rather "ways of reacting to and meeting such situations":

> Perhaps the boxer is dedicating his performance . . . , the mother . . . venerating the birth of her child as God's gift, . . . the parents . . . making their desires known to God, wanting the situation that has occasioned them to be met in him ["Religious Beliefs and Language-Games," p. 102].

In such cases, Phillips notes, the beliefs involved in the actions are not testable hypotheses. But we must further ask, What sort of beliefs *are* involved? Phillips offers some specific suggestions for the case of a mother who brings her newborn child and puts a garland on a statue of Mary:

> A mother may bring her newborn baby to the mother of Jesus in an act of veneration and thanksgiving: one mother greets another at the birth of a child. Connected with this act of greeting are a number of associated beliefs and attitudes: wonder and gratitude in face of new life, humility at being the means of bringing a child into the world, and, in this case, recognition of life as God's gift, the givenness of life [p. 104-5].

So far, however, this says nothing about the idea that protection is being sought for the child. What are we to make of this idea? According to Phillips, the key point is to realize that Mary is regarded as the paradigm of the virtues and attitudes that constitute holiness:

> Now when her protection is sought, the protection is the protection of her holiness; the mother wants the child's life to be orientated in these virtues. The first act in securing such an orientation is the bringing of the child to the Virgin. This orientation is what the believer would call the blessing of the Virgin Mary [p. 105].

Phillips' approach here is valuable because it reminds us that religious actions, including those frequently interpreted (even by those performing them) as means of influencing the course of future events, can have other sorts of significance. The mother who asks the Virgin to protect her child need not regard her petition as a means to making the child healthy, rich, etc. but rather as an expression of some fundamental attitudes toward life and as an initiation of the child into these attitudes. Because of this, the beliefs on which the action is based need not be hypotheses about what will happen to the child in the future. To this extent, the believer is not relying on any factual claims that need justifying evidence. However, Phillips has ignored other ways that factual beliefs are relevant to the faith of his believer. For the appropriateness of the mother's action surely depends on factual beliefs about Mary: that she became a mother, that she was a woman of outstanding virtue, etc. Consider a parallel case. We might imagine a neighborhood in which a new mother customarily takes her infant to visit and receive the blessing of all the other mothers who live on her block. If by accident she took the child to the house of a prostitute who had aborted her every pregnancy, her asking a blessing of this woman would be inappropriate, and precisely because it was based on a false factual belief about the woman's status. Similarly, if the Virgin Mary never existed or if her character has been substantially misrepresented by Catholic tradition, then a mother who presents a newborn baby to a statue of her is acting inappropriately because of a false factual belief.

Of course, it might be said that the woman's action is entirely symbolic, i.e., that the Blessed Virgin is nothing but a personification of a particular ideal of living, like the heroine of a didactic novel. But to say this is to misrepresent the woman's belief and action just as much as to say that it is a means of manipulating future events. We are, therefore, faced with a dilemma: either we interpret the woman's beliefs about Mary as factual, historical claims, in which case they surely need justification by the standard methods of the historian; or we avoid the need for such justification by misrepresenting the belief as having a merely symbolic content.

A similar dilemma emerges for Phillips' treatment of the Christian doctrine of the soul's immortality. He begins by noting the misunderstanding involved in talk of the soul as of a particular sort of thing that, along with the body, comprises a human being:

> If the soul were some quite distinct entity within a man, it would follow that whatever a man did would not affect it. But this is not how we speak of the soul. The relation between the soul and how a man lives is not a contingent one. It is when a man sinks to the depths of bestiality that someone might say that he had lost his soul. . . . Talk about the soul, then, is not talk about some strange sort of 'thing'. On the contrary, it is a kind of talk bound up with certain moral or religious reflections a man may make on the life he is leading. Once this is recognized, once one ceases to think of the soul as a thing, as some kind of incorporeal substance, one can be brought to see that in certain contexts talk about the soul *is* a way of talking about human beings.[14]

In particular, talk about the soul is talk about a human being's relation to *eternity*. This occurs first on the level of morality. As Plato and Kierkegaard have particularly emphasized, the demands of goodness are eternal demands in the sense that they call us beyond the cares of our temporal, day-to-day life. This is not to say that the life of morality, eternal life, is "some kind of appendage to human existence, something which happens *after* human life on earth is over." Rather, "eternal life is the reality of goodness, that in terms of which human life is to be assessed" (*Death and Immortality*, p. 48). Thus to speak of the soul as immortal is to speak of human life *sub specie aeternitatis*, as being evaluated by standards beyond those involved in a life of the prudent satisfaction of our desires and appetites. Eternal life is a quality of life that we are called to achieve even now; it has no essential reference to

a temporal extension, beyond death, of the period of time
through which we live:

> Questions about the immortality of the soul are seen not to be
> questions concerning the extent of a man's life, and in particular
> concerning whether that life can extend beyond the grave, but
> questions concerning the kind of life a man is living [p. 49].

Phillips sees a still deeper meaning for talk of the soul
and its immortality in the context of religion. Here it is
not merely a matter of participating in the eternal life of
ethical duty, but of sharing in the life of God himself.
Sharing in the life of God is a matter of "dying to the self,
seeing that all things are a gift from God, that nothing is
ours by right or necessity" (p. 55). Once again, immortality
in the sense of participation in the eternal divine life is not
a matter of a temporal extension of our time of life, but a
living of our temporal life in a way that "overcomes
death":

> The soul which is rooted in the mortal is the soul where the ego
> is dominant. . . . The immortality of the soul by contrast refers to
> a person's relation to the self-effacement and love of others in-
> volved in dying to the self. Death is overcome in that dying to the
> self is the meaning of the believer's life. As Plato says, "If this is
> true, and they have actually been looking forward to death all
> their lives, it would of course be absurd to be troubled when the
> thing comes for which they have so long been preparing and
> looking forward."[15]

Once again, Phillips' analysis is valuable because it calls
our attention to the defects of a tempting and common interpretation of Christian beliefs. The doctrine of immortality is frequently taken, by both believers and nonbelievers,
to mean that death is somehow only apparent (only the
death of the body) and that the life of temporal consciousness I had been leading up to my "final" moment continues
without interruption after death. (Or, at least, it is thought

that this life of temporal consciousness will be restored after a certain interval in the wake of the resurrection of the body.) Such an interpretation may well be philosophically defective because it ignores difficulties concerning personal identity; and it is certainly religiously defective because it ignores the deep qualitative differences between temporal and eternal life and the fact that the believer truly participates in eternal life even before death. Our immortality is not so much a matter of there being a guarantee of more of the same on the other side of the hill as it is a matter of a deeper meaning of what takes place on *this* side of the hill. This point is well put in a passage Phillips cites from Wittgenstein's *Tractatus*:

> Not only is there no guarantee of the temporal immortality of the human soul . . . ; but, in any case, this assumption completely fails to accomplish the purpose for which it has been intended. Or is some riddle solved by my surviving forever? Is not this eternal life itself as much of a riddle as our present life?[16]

However, as in the case of prayer, Phillips' analysis introduces its own characteristic distortion. In emphasizing the error of interpreting "eternal life" as a temporal continuation of our worldly life, Phillips ignores orthodox Christianity's insistence on the reality of eternal life quite apart from the vicissitudes of time. Immortality is, as Phillips says, our participation in God's life. But Christianity has traditionally taken this as a *personal* participation through which the same individual that previously existed in time comes to exist in eternity. Phillips may be right that this eternal existence cannot be a matter of an unending prolongation in time. But whatever eternal existence is, it is incompatible with any irrevocable cessation of existence. Accordingly, the Christian doctrine of personal immortality must at least mean that it will always be true to say that each human individual exists, even if it does not mean that all human individuals exist *at* all future times (hence, temporally). (Or, if we take immortality as contin-

gent on resurrection of the body, the Christian holds that
from some future time onward, it will always be true that
each human individual exists.) From this it is apparent that
the Christian doctrine of immortality expresses an important and controversial claim about the nature of human individuals, not just an attitude, interpretation, or evaluation.
As such it surely requires justification. If human beings are
regarded as empirical objects, knowable by ordinary sense
experience, then an empirical justification is called for. If
they are regarded as nonempirical objects, encountered by
some special nonsensory experience, then we need a justification on the basis of this sort of experience. In either
case, the dilemma is clear: either we acknowledge the
descriptive content of the doctrine of immortality and
thereby assume the burden of justifying it, or we misrepresent the doctrine by denying it any such content.

The dilemma posed by the two examples of prayer and
immortality are instances of the fundamental difficulty
facing the Wittgensteinian approach to religious belief: to
give beliefs a humanly meaningful content without making
them ordinary claims about ordinary objects and hence
putting them within the scope of standard methods of justification. Phillips himself has recognized this difficulty
and has formulated it as the need to avoid the extremes of
"externalism" and "internalism."[17] Externalism insists on
interpreting talk of God as on a par, semantically and epistemically, with talk of ordinary, nondivine objects. The
prime example of externalism is taking 'God exists' as a
hypothesis that there is a certain sort of unobservable
cause of certain observable effects. On such an interpretation, it is hard to see how believers can avoid the burden of
supporting their hypothesis with the evidence we would require of any other such hypothesis. Internalism, on the
other hand, sees talk of God as so semantically distinctive
that God's reality makes no difference to the events of our
world. So construed, religious beliefs are in principle immune to evaluation by methods of justification outside

religious systems. But, as Phillips notes, they then "begin to look like formal games, internally consistent but unconnected with the day-to-day lives of men and women."[18] The point is that if the meaning of religious claims is entirely *sui generis*, then there are no *religious* answers to our basic human questions about suffering, death, love, and hope. An answer must share a context of meaning with the question to which it responds. On the internalist construal, religion does not answer our questions; it changes the subject. This new subject may have its own fascination and value, but it does not tell us what we wanted to know. Of course sometimes the only adequate response to a question is one that transforms the question. If I ask, How can I avoid suffering?, the response might be: Ask rather how you can profit from suffering. But even here the response must be able to show itself the legitimate successor of the original question; and this requires continuity, if not sameness, of meaning. So one way or another, our talk about God must also be talk about our everyday world.

It might seem that to give up internalism is to give up the Wittgensteinian view of religious beliefs as properly groundless. For if religious claims are about our world, surely they are open to evaluation by our ordinary canons of evidence and argument. Suppose for example, we ask, Why is there suffering?, and entertain the religious response: There is no suffering, only the illusion of it, because God is the sole reality and He includes only joy. Surely we can and must reject this answer on the grounds that we know from our common experience that suffering is not an illusion but a persistent reality. And if believers reply that they are not speaking of suffering in our ordinary mundane sense, then they have simply evaded the question at hand.

The response to this objection is that there is a difference between grounding a belief and defending it; that is, between providing reasons sufficient to warrant a belief and responding to objections raised against it. In this regard, the Wittgensteinian approach has often erred by emphasizing only the similarities between fundamental religious beliefs and prototype groundless beliefs such as 'I have two hands,' 'The future will be like the past,' and 'Material objects do not just disappear without any cause'. Such beliefs not only need no grounds — that is, we are entitled to accept them without evidence for their truth — but also need no defense — that is, there are no objections or difficulties that need be overcome before we are entitled to them. But needing no grounds and needing no defense are not the same. It may be, for example, that I am entitled to a belief only if I can show it is not self-contradictory and that, once this is shown, I have no need to provide any positive support for it. If religion is to have relevance to our everyday lives, it must have implications about everyday realities such as love and death. And these implications have to be defended against claims that they are at odds with what we know about these realities quite apart from religious considerations. Defending religious beliefs in this way will require appeals to ordinary methods of justification, but such appeals will not amount to a justification of the beliefs being defended.

A corollary is that the idea that religious beliefs can be justified but not falsified is wrong. Any humanly relevant religious belief is open to refutation; but, if the Wittgensteinian suggestion is correct, it cannot be justified. Accordingly, the groundlessness of fundamental religious beliefs does not require their internalist isolation from all rational criticism. The claim of groundlessness implies only that the belief is immune to the criticism that one is not entitled to a religious belief because one has no sufficient evidence for it.

The above considerations, however, do no more than clear the ground for an account of the meaning of religious language that will both exhibit it as of consequence for our lives and show the inappropriateness of demands for justification of fundamental religious claims.

Before turning to this question, let me sum up briefly the main thrust of our discussion so far. The Wittgensteinian approach to religious belief can be characterized by three central elements: (1) a methodological injunction to examine religious discourse from the inside, without the imposition of external (e.g., scientific, philosophical) criteria of meaning and truth; (2) a fundamental epistemological point (most prominent in *On Certainty*) that all justifications must be based on "framework principles" that define the context in which questions of justification may be raised and for which the question of justification cannot be properly raised; (3) an analysis of the nature of religious language (in accord with [1]), showing that fundamental religious beliefs are framework principles (in the sense of [2]).

Wittgensteinians sometimes give the impression that they think the issue of the justification of religious belief is settled by either (1) or (2) taken separately. Thus, it sometimes seems to be assumed that any raising of the justification question is *a fortiori* an illegitimate imposition of external standards, or that religious belief so obviously corresponds to an autonomous framework of living, experiencing, and thinking that, once we realize the special status of framework principles, the question of the justification of fundamental religious beliefs disappears. In fact, however, it is not obvious that questions about the justification of fundamental religious beliefs always assume inapplicable external standards or that religious forms of life are autonomous in a way that excludes the meaningful raising of such questions of justification. Rather, the inappropriateness of the justification issue must be shown through (3); that is, by giving a detailed account of religious language (talk of God) that exhibits the autonomy of the religious mode of discourse and hence the inappropriateness of the methods of justification we use in other contexts, for the evaluation of fundamental religious beliefs.

4. The Groundlessness of Belief and the
Nature of Religious Language

Since religious language is essentially about God, our question amounts to that of the meaning of talk about God. Specifically, the Wittgensteinian case requires an account of "God-talk" that shows it to be sufficiently distinctive to avoid externalism but not so idiosyncratic as to lead to internalism.[19] Both Norman Malcolm and D. Z. Phillips hold that the key to such an account is the recognition of the *necessity* of God's existence. Phillips, for example, says:

> Because religious believers want to say that there is 'something' called God, it has been assumed that it ought to be possible to establish whether this 'something' exists, in the way in which we establish the truth or falsity of certain matters of fact when there is some uncertainty about them. But what is the case is not established in the same way in every context. Consider, for example, how we would establish whether it is the case that I have a speck in my eye, a picture in my mind, a pain in my head, a one in six chance of getting a job, been reading a book, been reading a good book, and so on. Or again, are we asking the same thing when we ask whether unicorns, numbers, magic, or electrons, exist? All these are 'something,' but what the 'something' comes to will vary with the case in question and so will the method of establishing whether or not that 'something' is the case. In the case of the 'something' men call God, it is clear that it will not dance to the tune appropriate to many of the ways in which we talk of things *which may or may not be the case*. . . . Most believers are not prepared to say that God might not exist. The point is not that *as a matter of fact* God will always exist, but that it *makes no sense* to say that God might not exist. The idea of God is such that the possibility of the non-existence of God is logically precluded. It follows from this that God's existence is not *contingent*.[20]

However, this suggestion is not without difficulties. The

first concerns Phillips' assumption that methods appropriate for establishing the existence of contingent things will not be appropriate for establishing the existence of a necessary God. Such a claim is plausible for the abstract necessary entities (numbers, propositions, essences) posited by Platonic ontologists, because such entities exercise no (efficient) causal influence in the world and our ordinary empirical methods of justification typically argue from effects to causes. But in the case of God we have a necessary being that is, somehow or another, causally related to the world (e.g., as its creator). It may well be maintained that the sort of causal relation obtaining between God and his world is very different from the causal relations presupposed by, say, hypothetico-deductive inferences. But merely noting God's necessity says nothing about this issue.

This last claim may seem to be false. As Phillips emphasizes, because God is necessary, his existence entails nothing about how the contingent events of the world will go. "The believer cannot expect one thing rather than another in the world of events".[21] This point follows from God's necessity for the following reason: to exist necessarily is to exist in all possible worlds; so if God's existence entailed the actuality of one possible world rather than another (i.e., contingent events going one way rather than another), then he would not exist necessarily. Accordingly, we cannot undertake a crucial test of God's existence by finding some contingent events the occurrence of which verifies his existence and the nonoccurrence of which refutes it. Given this, it might be argued that God's necessity does entail that he cannot be causally related to the world the way contingent causes are, and hence that the hypothetico-deductive mode of argument appropriate for establishing the existence of contingent causes is not applicable to God.

However, such an argument is based on the false assumption that the hypothetico-deductive mode of argumentation involves crucial experiments. As Lakatos, for example, has pointed out, this is not so, because "even a

most respected scientific theory, like Newton's dynamics
and theory of gravitation, may fail to forbid any observable
state of affairs."[22] The reason is that a scientific theory
will typically entail that one observable state of affairs
rather than another will obtain only on the assumption
that a specific set of factors are the *only* relevant influences
on the situation in question. Thus, Newton's law of gravitation entails that a planet will move around the sun in an
elliptical orbit only if there is no force acting on the planet
other than the sun's gravitational attraction. Because there
will generally be no observations capable of establishing
the negative claim that there are no other factors (including ones not yet conceptualized by scientific theories)
operative in a given situation, the truth or falsity of scientific hypotheses will not in general be determinable by crucial experiments. So the possibility of a crucial experiment
does not distinguish the evaluation of scientific hypotheses
from the evaluation of 'God exists'. The two differ logically in that the former, but not the latter, has contingent
entailments. But this logical difference does not directly
translate into a difference in the methods of justification
appropriate to scientific hypotheses and 'God exists'. This
is not to say there are no such differences; but just that, if
there are, they do not follow in an obvious way from
God's necessity.

A second difficulty for Phillips' view is this: even if we
assume that ordinary methods of empirical justification
are not relevant to 'God exists', it surely does not follow
that the methods of justification ordinarily employed for
purported necessary truths (i.e., methods of logical and
conceptual analysis) are not relevant. We could not, for
example, plausibly claim that the beliefs that there are
transfinite numbers or a Form of Triangularity are properly groundless because they are about necessary existents.

In this connection, it is instructive to note Phillips'
attitude toward the ontological argument, which purports
to be a conceptual demonstration of God's existence.

Although he thinks there are obvious flaws in what has come to be called Anselm's "first" version of the argument, he is much more impressed by the "second" version as formulated in Malcolm's famous article. Not that he thinks it grounds religious belief by proving God's existence; but it does, he thinks, decisively clarify the meaning of belief and disbelief in God. This is because it shows that anyone who admits that the concept 'God' is self-consistent must also admit that God exists. There is no middle ground where we can say that God *might* exist, though he in fact does not or we do not know whether or not he does. This does not exclude atheism and agnosticism as alternatives, but it does show that they are viable only if they claim that the concept of God is self-contradictory or meaningless, or that we do not know whether or not it is self-contradictory or meaningless. Thus, with regard to atheism Phillips says:

> . . . if the atheist says in his heart, 'There is not God', where this makes it logically permissible to say (though it may be false as a matter of fact), 'There may have been a God in the past, and there may be a God in the future', so far, he has not even spoken of, let alone rejected, the idea of an eternal God. . . . But there are other forms of atheism. The atheist may say that the idea of a necessary being is self-contradictory. This is arguable. . . . Again, atheism may take another form, one which, to my mind, is the most genuine indication of what atheism is. I am thinking of atheism as the recognition that religion means nothing to one. . . . It is the form of atheism summed up in the phrases, 'I shouldn't call myself religious', 'Religion has no meaning for me'. To this latter expression of unbelief there is no philosophical objection.[23]

Of course there would be a philosophical objection to atheism (and to agnosticism) if we could prove that the concept 'God' is self-consistent. Why then, we might ask, does Phillips continue to insist that there are no methods available for grounding the belief that God exists? Couldn't the relevant ground be supplied by a philosophical proof that 'God' is self-consistent? And should we not with-hold judgment on the question of God's existence until the concept is proved consistent or inconsistent? Here Phillips follows Malcolm in claiming that there is no sense to a request for a general proof of the consistency of the concept of God. It is possible to meet particular objections to the concept's consistency but, in Malcolm's words, "I do not understand what it would mean to demonstrate *in general,* and not in respect to any particular reasoning, that the concept is not self-contradictory."[24] But why should this be so? Of course there can be no *absolute* proof of consistency in the sense of a proof that made no assumptions about the consistency of other concepts. But, as is frequently done in mathematics, it is entirely possible to supply cogent *relative* consistency proofs by showing that a given concept can be defined in terms of other concepts, the consistency of which is not in question. Surely there is nothing in the necessity of God's existence (any more than there is in the necessity of a transfinite number's existence) that excludes this possibility. Accordingly, there is nothing in the fact of God's necessary existence that excludes the possibility of a consistency proof and so entails the inapplicability of techniques of logical and conceptual analysis to the justification of belief in God.

The fault, of course, may be due simply to the inadequacy of Phillips's account of the distinctive nature of God-talk. But no Wittgensteinian philosopher of religion has done even as much as Phillips to develop such an account. In spite of their emphasis on the need to pay close attention to the distinctive features of religious language, Wittgensteinians have done very little toward developing a detailed account of the nature of talk about God. For this reason, Wittgensteinian philosophy of religion remains embarrassingly programmatic. We are told that a proper understanding of the distinctive features of religious language will show the inappropriateness of demands to justify religious claims. But Wittgensteinians have not given the detailed account of religious language needed to evaluate this claim.

Such accounts are, nonetheless, available. Traditional Christian theology, for example, provides us with very rich discussions of the analogical uses of language appropriate to talk about God. Such discussions provide an excellent basis for evaluating the Wittgensteinian thesis about justification, for they allow us to assess the thesis in the context of a full-blown account of the distinctive features of religious language. Accordingly, reflection on the Wittgensteinian view of justification leads naturally to reflection on traditional theological theories of talk about God. (This conclusion fits in with Phillips's view that questions about the meaning of religious language are properly treated by theology, not philosophy; see *Faith and Philosophical Inquiry,* pp. 5 ff.)

Of course, our evaluation of the Wittgensteinian thesis will depend on the particular account of religious language that we choose as the basis of our discussion. On the other hand, it is hardly practical for us to settle here the issue of the most adequate account of religious language. Accordingly, I propose to evaluate the Wittgensteinian thesis on the basis of a version of a traditional account that is *prima facie* maximally favorable to the thesis: David Burrell's interpretation of Thomas Aquinas' doctrine of analogy. This will be the subject of the next chapter.

2. Aquinas on Religious Language

1. Introduction

The Wittgensteinian idea that demands to justify fundamental religious beliefs are inappropriate would surely seem to find most support in accounts of religious language that emphasize the incomprehensibility and ineffability of God. To the extent that God escapes our conceptual and linguistic categories, it would seem that claims about him will be beyond our ordinary methods of justification. But although the incomprehensibility and ineffability of God are emphasized by many religious thinkers in almost all traditions, it is difficult to find nontrivial accounts of these topics that do not fall into incoherence. Consider, for example, the suggestion, popular among contemporary theologians, that none of our concepts are applicable to God. In this bald form, the suggestion is certainly absurd. As Alvin Plantinga argues in a recent paper:

> It is a piece of sheer confusion to say that there is such a person as God, but none of our concepts apply to him. . . . If our concepts do not apply to God, then our concepts of being loving, almighty, wise, creator and Redeemer do not apply to him, in which case he is not loving, almighty, wise, a creator or a Redeemer. He won't have any of the properties Christians ascribe to him. In fact he won't have any of the properties of which we have concepts. He will not have such properties as self-identity,

existence, and being either a material object or an immaterial object, these being properties of which we have concepts. Indeed, he won't have the property of being the referent of the term 'God', or any other term; our concept *being the referent of a term* does not apply to him. The fact is this being won't have any properties at all, since our concept of having at least one property does not apply to him. But how could there be such a thing? How could there be a being that didn't exist, wasn't self-identical, wasn't either a material or an immaterial object, didn't have any properties? Does any of this make even marginal sense? It is clearly quite impossible that there be a thing to which none of our concepts apply.[1]

One might reply that to say none of our concepts applies to God is not to say that God lacks the properties expressed by those concepts but that no meaningful statements can be made that either assert or deny such properties to God. But this would mean that all statements about God are meaningless, which would amount to a surrender to the strongest form of skepticism about religion.

Another suggestion is that all statements about God are false. But this too is absurd. For if all statements about God were false, it would follow that all statements about God were also true: every statement about God is the negation of some other statement about God; hence, on the hypothesis that all statements about God are false, every statement about God is the negation of a false statement and hence is a true statement. So the suggestion that all statements about God are false is self-contradictory. If it is suggested rather that no statement about God is either true or false, this is just to concede once again that talk of God is meaningless. A proper doctrine of the divine incomprehensibility must acknowledge our capacity to make some meaningful and true statements about God.

On the other hand, weaker construals of the divine incomprehensibility do not seem strong enough to support the Wittgensteinian thesis. It might, for example, be said that the incomprehensibility of God means simply that 'God' can be given no essential definition (i.e., no definition expressing the divine nature). But this is true of many terms (e.g., basic sensory predicates) and by no means requires that claims about the objects denoted by such terms admit of no justification. Similarly, if incomprehensibility means only that our knowledge of God is always incomplete or that our assertions about him must be always tentative, we have said nothing of him that we cannot say of many other realities.

What the Wittgensteinian needs, then, is an account of God-talk that avoids the extremes of both incoherence and triviality. The most obvious place to look for such an account is in traditional doctrines of analogy, which emphasize both the uniqueness and the meaningfulness of talk about God. However, standard interpretations of analogical predication (e.g., by Thomists such as Gilson and Maritain) are developed so as to make the project of proving God's existence (by the five and other ways) entirely legitimate. So they are unlikely to be congenial to the Wittgensteinian. There is, however, one recent interpretation of Aquinas' doctrine of analogy that is *prima facie* well suited as a basis for the Wittgensteinian thesis — that proposed by David Burrell.[2] Because this is also one of the fullest and most sophisticated discussions of God-talk in the recent literature, I shall examine it in some detail. In focusing on this discussion, I am not assuming that it is either the best interpretation of Aquinas' texts or even an ultimately coherent account of religious language. I am interested in it as the best example I have been able to find of a well-developed view of God-talk that seems congenial to the Wittgensteinian thesis about justification.

2. Burrell's Interpretation of Aquinas

According to Burrell, Aquinas presents a view for which human cognition of God is constituted by complementary moments of denial and intimation. The moments of denial (points along the *via remotionis*) represent all that we can *know,* in a strict sense of the term, about God. Here Aquinas formulates claims "which deny [of God] a specific formal feature of objects as we know them," and "the arguments proceed with logical precision" (*Exercises in Religious Understanding,* p. 89). The moments of intimation (points along the *via eminentiae*) do not represent knowledge but attempts to turn "our very inability to know God into a fruitful piece of information."[3] Burrell characterizes this path of Aquinas' inquiry in Wittgensteinian terms:

> Aquinas probes the possibilities of different ways of thinking and speaking to test for intimations which the outright denial might have opened up. He makes an implicit appeal to a quality of experience, a form of life which could prepare someone to adopt a way of speaking quite different from that adapted to physical objects [p. 88].

Our denials about God are often regarded straightforwardly as literally true negative assertions about God; thus, God is not a body, not changeable, and the like. Burrell, however, sees these denials in a much more radical way. In Aquinas' treatment, every denial of a property to God is made because, in one way or another, it connotes *composition* (e.g., of matter and form, genus and species, substance and accident, or essence and existence), which can never be properly attributed to God. Now, for Aquinas, the logical form of any statement presupposes composition in its subject (e.g., a subject-predicate form presumes a distinction between a thing and its properties). Consequently, the true significance of the *via remotionis* is to deny the possibility of making well-formed statements about God. Far from yielding literally true negative statements about God, the moment of denial shows that we cannot properly say *anything* about God. What we know here is just that we cannot know God.

If this is the upshot of the moment of denial, one wonders what can possibly be left for the moment of intimation. It might seem that the only possibility is some recourse to a prelinguistic experience of God that may perhaps be evoked by language but in no way expressed by it. But to define religion in terms of such experience would be to abandon any real commitment to religious *beliefs*, which must be assertions of what is true, not merely devices for triggering certain experiences. (I pass over the many difficulties in the very notion of a prelinguistic experience.) However, according to Burrell, Aquinas sees another possibility. If we cannot properly speak of God, then we must speak of him improperly. Indeed, analogical predication is precisely the art of expressing truths that cannot be expressed properly. The idea of our being able to express a truth improperly depends on Aquinas' distinction between *mode of signifying (modus significandi)* and *what is meant (res significata)*. Burrell explains the distinction:

> *What is signified* does not refer directly to an existing object, of course, but rather to an intentional fact: it is *what we intend* by saying what we do. The *manner of signifying* is the way we put what we say; more precisely, the expression refers to the various entanglements in which we find ourselves by putting it that way. The more skilled we become in recognizing these entanglements and in extricating ourselves from them by bringing forth variant expressions, the more accurately do we succeed in saying what we mean. There is no magic way to deliver what is meant except by expressing it [p. 127].

Accepting this distinction allows for the possibility, crucial for discourse about God, of saying what is correct but saying it incorrectly.

The idea of saying what is correct incorrectly has an air

of paradox about it, but there are many instances of it. For example, the statements of small children (and others just learning English) are often either literally false or meaningless because of grammatical errors but nonetheless express truths (e.g., "Mama go car", "I don't see no dog"). More elaborately, entire systems of incorrect expressions of truths can be readily imagined. Consider, for example, a group of people, attending (by some chance) the Rose Bowl game, who know nothing at all about football but have a good grasp of baseball. In their efforts to describe what they are seeing, they might well be led to make deviant but effective use of the language of baseball, speaking perhaps of the player who throws or runs with the ball on a given play as the "batter," describing first downs as "hits," touchdowns as "home runs," the interception of a first-down pass as a "triple play," and so on. With enough refinement, such a language could express a good many, though probably not all, of the truths about what was going on in the game, although the manner of expression would be entirely wrong. Thus, someone might say, "The same player batted four times in a row, got hits the first three times, and then hit into a triple play" — a statement rife with literal absurdities but nonetheless expressing the truth that the quarterback threw passes for three successive first downs and then was intercepted.

This football example is also helpful because it shows that it is possible to assess the truth-value of analogical statements without reliance on "translations" into literal language. Those learning English are assured of the truth of their deviant utterances by the approval of experienced speakers who know what the statements "really mean." But our novice football fans can, with enough experience, make sound judgments as to the probable truth of their statements entirely on their own. Those of us who wish to speak of God must also forge our own criteria for the veracity of our utterances. We have no access to a literal translation because no such translation is possible.

This leads to the crucial question of how standards for the veracity of talk about God can be devised. According to Burrell, Aquinas initiates such standards by exploiting our very inability to make literally true statements about God. We can express our knowledge of the essential properties of finite objects by using the predication schema:

To be ＿＿＿＿＿＿ is to be ＿＿＿＿＿＿.

Thus, to be a human being is to be rational, to be a square is to be four-sided. Because God lacks composition, this schema cannot be applied to him. Expressions of the form, "to be God is to be ＿＿＿＿＿＿," though well formed in surface grammar, are inappropriate to God, who has no properties (essential or accidental) distinct from himself. However, God's very lack of all composition suggests a deviant form of expression that is appropriate to him. For among the compositions lacking in God is that of essence and existence; that is, in God there is no distinction between *what he is* (his essence) and *the fact that he is* (his existence or, in Burrell's literal translation of Aquinas' *esse,* his to-be). Since where there is no distinction there is identity, we must say that God's essence is his existence; or, putting it in a way that fits the above predication schema:

To be God is to be to-be.[4]

This expression is ill formed because it uses the substantive "to-be" where only a predicate adjective (e.g., "wise") is appropriate. Or, to make the point in a more philosophical way, the expression treats existence (= to be) as a descriptive predicate. Nonetheless, the expression is a correct claim about God because it conveys the truth that he has no composition of essence and existence.

There is an obvious objection to the above procedure. The expression "to be God is to be to-be" has been presented as, so far, the only correct statement we can make about God and its correctness has been said to require its grammatical impropriety. But it seems that the very construction of this expression has made use of statements about God that are allegedly correct and properly formed as well. In particular, we developed "to be God is to be to-be" by applying the claim, "God is not composite" to the particular case of composition of essence and existence. But it would seem that "God is not composite" is itself a well-formed statement expressing a truth about God. If so, the entire procedure of developing an analogical language to speak of God is based on a literal truth about God, and the claim that we can formulate only analogical truths about God is self-defeating.

However, Burrell might claim this objection is wrong because "God is not composite" must be read not as an object-language statement about God but as a metalinguistic statement about the word "God." It means: there are no well-formed statements of the form "God is P" (where P is any descriptive predicate). If we insist on the object-language reading, then the truth of the metalinguistic statement I have proposed as the correct reading shows that "God is not composite" is not well formed.

But the objection can be pressed further by asking for our warrant for "God is not composite," taken in a metalinguistic sense. For it would seem that the basis for the statement must be some information about God himself. Indeed, according to Burrell, Aquinas concludes that God is not composite because God is "the first cause of all things." (The argument is that composition is the mark of a caused being and so cannot be found in the necessarily uncaused first cause.) Surely, it might be objected, we cannot read "God is the first cause of all things" as a metalinguistic statement. But, Burrell might reply, we can and must; for, in the present discussion, "God is the first cause of all things" is not a description of God but a statement of how the word "God" is used in our language (hence a nominal, not a real, definition). More fully, the situation is this: the philosopher notices that, in many contexts, the word "God" is used in such a way that it is appropriate to substitute for it the expression "the first cause of all things." Focusing on this expression the philosopher asks if there are any predicates that might be combined with it to yield well-formed descriptive statements. In other words, are there any well-formed expressions of the form "the first cause of all things is P"? The answer is no on the grounds that, if there were, we would have to assert "the first cause of all things is composite," since predication entails composition in the subject of predication. Asserting this would require asserting "the first cause of all things is caused," because composition is the mark of the caused. And, since in this context "first cause" means "uncaused cause", this would amount to asserting "the uncaused cause of all things is caused." Because avoidance of this sort of contradiction is a necessary condition on any intelligible use of "the first cause of all things," it follows that we can intelligibly use this expression only if we admit that it cannot be properly used as a subject of predication; i.e., that there are no well-formed expressions of the form "the first cause of all things is P." The derivation of this conclusion thus relies only on metalinguistic truths about our use of certain expressions, not on any substantive claims about God.

Starting from the basic formula "to be God is to be to-be," Aquinas is able to develop an entire system of God-talk, by developing expressions equivalent to the basic formula. For example, he notes that as first cause God is the source of any perfection that could be possessed by a creature. From this he concludes that God must in some sense contain all these perfections; and, because this cannot be a matter of his having them as properties (for this would involve composition), we must say simply that he is all perfections, that for him to be is to be perfect. From this it follows that "to be God is to be to-be" is equivalent to "to be God is to be perfect." Similar arguments establish the equivalence of the basic formula to "to be God is to be unchangeable," "to be God is to be infinite," etc.

Of course these arguments rely on principles of Aquinas' metaphysical system (e.g., the claim that a cause must contain the reality of its effects is based on an Aristotelian account of causality); but it is reasonable to think that alternative metaphysical viewpoints could generate similar systems of discourse about God. In fact, as Burrell notes, Aquinas frequently shows how his points can be made in the language of a Platonic-Augustinian metaphysics of participation. So even if we might have reservations about the particular way Aquinas develops a language appropriate for speaking of God, it remains plausible that such a language is possible.

A much more fundamental difficulty concerns our understanding of such a language. Burrell says that in speaking of God we "say what we mean without pretending to know what we mean when we say it of God. In fact, it is precisely by realizing that we do *not* know what it is we are saying that we are licensed to say what we do say" (p. 131). What is the point of this puzzling statement? It derives from Burrell's belief that, although we can construct a language appropriate for talk about God, we have no ability to *use* this language. This can be elucidated by reference to Sellars' distinction between the moves of a language-game and the entry- and exit-transition (see ch. 1, above). Our construction of a language for speaking of God has merely provided a set of rules governing intra-linguistic moves. It has not provided us with the entry and exit rules needed to use the language in the sense of employing it to mediate between our experiences and our actions. We are like someone who has memorized a textbook on wine-tasting but has never tasted wine.

Further, it seems there is no possibility of our coming to learn entry- and exit-transitions for our language of God. For learning this means coming to have experiences of the object talked about by the language, and there is no question of our experiencing God. So it is not just that we have never tasted wine, but that we have no sense of taste. But if we are incapable of *using*, in a full-blooded sense, our language about God, how could this language – and the religious belief expressed by it – be of any importance in our lives? It would seem that at best it could be a formal game with no practical consequences beyond the enjoyment it might occasionally provide or the emotions that might be stimulated by playing it. (This problem is the counterpart of the Wittgensteinian's problem of avoiding internalism.)

Responding to this objection requires explicating the moment of intimation in our knowledge of God. So far everything we have said has derived from the basic denial of all composition in God. But though these derivations can be carried out rigorously (within a given metaphysical framework), it seems that there is a fundamental sense in which we do not understand them, because they have no ties to the experiences and actions of our lives. A believer whose faith went no further than the moment of denial would really be in no different position than the unbeliever we spoke of in chapter 1, who knew the moves of the religious language-game but could not understand its entry- and exit-transitions.

So if the present account of religious language is to be compatible with genuine belief, we must be able to exhibit a realm of experience that will provide the requisite understanding of the religious language-game. This realm will be the locus of what Burrell calls our intimations of God.

The possibility of "intimations" arises because the terms of our language for talking of God are also terms of the other language-games in which we participate. Thus, "perfect" has a variety of pragmatic, moral, and aesthetic senses, quite apart from its role in talk of God. Further, although we do not know how to use (in the full sense) these terms when they are part of language about God, we do know how to use them in other contexts. This knowledge, Burrell argues, enables us to claim that there could be a use of the terms in talk about God:

> Although *we* do not possess the use, we *do* possess skills requisite to reflect on the uses we do have and to recognize a set of features common enough to be gathered into a structure (or syntax). That capacity allows us to state that expressions of the sort *could be* used of God, by one who would know how to do it. We do not know how, hence we can never know precisely what we mean when we license these terms to be used of God [p. 130].

He illustrates his point for the case of the application of the term "living" to God:

> . . . the believer . . . wants to address the living God. Yet he would be the first to acknowledge that even the term of address shades into unknown reaches. He does not pretend to know what he means when he says it, knowing that the living God realizes *life* in a totally different way than he can grasp. Nonetheless, there are analogies — leads that one can follow — which allow us to use our own experiences to intimate what God's life might be like. These are expressly exploratory and tentative, and always open to correction as we acquire greater skill in ordering the uses we do possess of those expressions called "perfections" [p. 131].

Put in this way, Burrell's position seems to me open to two criticisms. First, the idea that there is a use of our language about God that we humans do not possess but that might be possessed by someone strikes me as untenable. This language is, for all its peculiarities, *our* language, constructed by us; and if we cannot use it, it is hard to see how anyone else (angels? God himself?) could. Second, and more important, the mere in principle possibility of a usage of the language is not sufficient to respond to the objection that a language we cannot use can have no importance in our lives. The fact that the language could be used shows merely that it could make a difference for someone, not that it makes a difference for us.

Accordingly, an account of religious language that takes

it seriously must show how we can actually use it; that is, how we can properly describe our experience in it and direct our action by means of it. The problem is to show this, given that we can neither experience nor act upon the divine object of this language. I think the way to a solution can be found in Burrell's examples of intimation, which seem to me to suggest what his explicit account of intimation omits. Consider his treatment of our understanding of the claim that to be God is to be perfect. After deriving this principle, Aquinas applies it to a discussion of the question, "Can creatures be said to resemble God?" He answers that they do resemble God just because they exist: "for precisely as things possessing existence they resemble the primary and universal source of all existence" (cited, p. 102). Burrell comments that this assertion is "improper if not nonsensical" inasmuch as existence is not a *characteristic* that could be the basis for a resemblance between two things. But, he suggests, Aquinas is "speaking with a deliberate impropriety" (i.e., analogically). But what is the point of the impropriety? Burrell tells us:

> Aquinas is trying to lead us on to some intimation of . . . the difference each thing makes simply by being. We might want to speak of its "intrinsic worth" prior to any achievement. He is saying that each thing most resembles God simply in that it is, and in doing what is its thing to do. This terse observation in effect invites us to assume a more contemplative posture toward the world if we wish to know what God is like. For taking each thing as an object-for-me accepts its very being as a mere presupposition, and overlooks the "thing it does" in favor of what it might do for me [p. 103].

Having said that God's perfection consists simply in the fact that he is, we are led to reflect on what this might tell us about the finite beings of our experience. It tells us that we might try thinking of the perfection of such beings in terms of the mere fact that they exist, rather than in terms of what they have done or the purposes for which we might use them. Thinking in this way may well have important results: we may experience the world in a new dimension and take a significantly different attitude toward it.

It seems to me that this very perceptively presented example shows precisely the way in which we can use our language about God: not to incorporate God as an object of our experience and action but to provide opportunities for new modes of experience and action in relation to the objects of our world. This does not mean that our talk of God is really only talk about the world. We come to say new things about the world because of what we have said about God. On the other hand, it might be objected that we are not really using our talk of God, because we are still not experiencing him. To answer this objection, we need to reflect more carefully than we have on what might be meant by an experience of God. If "experiencing God" means somehow directly apprehending (e.g., by an intellectual intuition) the divine essence, then, for Aquinas, an experience of God is simply impossible for us. All our experience involves the classification of the experienced object under concepts; and, since concepts express properties, any object that can be so classified is composite. However, there is another sense in which Aquinas might allow that we can experience God. This is by experiencing his presence in the events of our world. Our development of a language for talking about God can, as we have just seen, lead us to new sorts of experiences of finite objects. Because what such experiences reveal about these objects is similar to what we have said of God, it is proper to speak of them as also revealing God.

Here I think Burrell is a bit misleading. He tends to speak as though reflection on the objects of our experience gives us some idea of what God is like (see the last indented quotation above). But it is rather that reflection on what we "know" (i.e., are entitled to assert) of God that gives us some idea of how the objects of our experience are like him. In any case, it is these experiences of creatures as like God that allow for transitions into our language about God. For example, a man who has been accustomed to see his children only as sources of pride or disappointment to him may, in a precious and perhaps transforming moment, experience the inestimable value of their mere reality, quite apart from how they please or displease him. Such a man can rightly say that he has seen God in his children. A religious form of life provides the training that enables the believer to have such experiences, to appropriately express them in religious language, and to respond to the truths so expressed with appropriate actions.

We have been discussing how the principle "to be God is to be perfect" might have a use for us. Similarly, Burrell suggests uses for other statements about God. Thus, "to be God is to be good" might lead us to see how persons can be of great moral importance for others, not by performing actions on their behalf but just by being themselves. Morality, accordingly, may be as much or more a matter of what we are as of what we do. Likewise, Burrell suggests that a realization that "to be God is to be eternal" may direct us to aspects of our inner experience in which we are aware of a kind of reality to which the categories of process (motion and rest, etc.) are not applicable. And the fact that "to be God is to be one" can lead us to an appreciation of the "integrity" of all things.

Development of these ideas can show — and, in the Christian tradition, has shown — how talk of an incomprehensible God (i.e., a God of whom no literally true descriptive statements can be made) can have profound effects on the way we experience, think about, and act toward ourselves and the world around us. This makes a strong case for the possibility of providing an account of the divine incomprehensibility that avoids the internalist irrelevance of an entirely isolated and autonomous system of discourse. Further, the fact that Burrell is able to present this account as a plausible interpretation of so central a Christian thinker as Thomas Aquinas suggests that it is not a distortion of the historical meaning of Christianity. It appears then that Burrell's interpretation of Aquinas provides a viable account of religious language that is extremely favorable to the Wittgensteinian suggestion that it is not appropriate to seek a justification for fundamental religious beliefs. For, although the account avoids internalism, it nonetheless makes God a unique entity to whom none of our predicates can be properly applied. Rather, we can speak of God only in a language peculiar to him, a language whose meaning we can only indirectly intimate. It is hard to imagine any account, short of sheer internalism, that goes further toward insulating claims about God from the justificatory canons that govern ordinary discourse. In the following section, however, I hope to show that even on this account the claim that God exists is open to and requires justification.

3. Is Belief in God Properly Groundless?

Giving a ground for religious belief means, ultimately, giving reasons for the existence of the God who is the object of that belief. There seem to be just three ways of establishing the existence of anything – namely, by showing: (1) that its existence is a conceptual truth (i.e., that denying its existence leads to contradiction); (2) that it is the immediate object of a veridical experience (as, e.g., when we know a tree exists just because we see it); (3) that it is the best explanation of some fact that is in need of explanation. Of course, arguments of all three sorts have been traditional in cases for religious belief. The question before us is whether any of them are appropriate, given the above Thomistic account of the meaning of statements about God.

(1) Here, of course, the question is whether there might be a sound ontological argument for God's existence.

Critiques of such arguments have traditionally focused on the related difficulties of moving logically from mental existence to actual existence and of treating "existence" as a descriptive predicate. In my view, Plantinga's recent version of the argument escapes the traditional difficulties and, indeed, successfully establishes the existence of God, *given* the premise that the existence of a divine being is logically possible.[5] However, I believe the Thomistic account of our talk of God excludes the possibility of ever establishing this key premise. If so, it cuts off all ontological arguments, because they all depend on the assumption that God's existence is possible.

The difficulty arises in this way: to prove that "God exists" is logically possible, it is necessary to prove that 'God' is a logically consistent concept. Now there are just two ways to prove that a concept is logically consistent. The first is to show that there is something to which it applies (that it is instantiated). In the case at hand, this procedure would obviously be question-begging. The second way is (a) to express the concept in terms of other concepts that are instantiated (and hence consistent) and (b) to show that these concepts are mutually consistent. It is the first step that poses the problem. For to show that concepts applicable to God are instantiated by beings other than him would require showing that there are predicates applicable to God and to creatures in the same sense. But, on the Thomistic account, there are no such predicates. For any predicate P that is applicable to God must be understood in such a way that to be P is to be; and this can never be true of a predicate applicable to a creature. Accordingly, the Thomistic account of talk of God leaves no room for a proof of the possibility of his existence and so excludes any ontological argument showing that "God exists" is a conceptual truth.

(2) We saw above that talk of God is relevant to the believer's life in virtue of experiences of the world that reveal it as similar to God; and we even said that such experiences

are experiences of God. Can, then, the believer appeal to them as evidence of the reality of Aquinas' God? I think not. As we also saw, the believer experiences God only in the sense of "seeing him in" creatures; that is, seeing that there are truths about creatures similar to truths about God. What is literally experienced is just creatures and truths about them. These truths reveal God via their similarity to truths about him only on the assumption that the latter are indeed truths about an actual God, hence only on the assumption that God exists. There is a helpful parallel to this situation in the idea of "seeing an artist's character in his works." If we already know that the author of a novel has certain characteristic traits, then we can readily see these traits in his books. Thus, if I am reading a novel by a colleague who, I know, yearns for a return to the Middle Ages, I can immediately see this trait in his cynical portrayal of modern foibles. But if I know nothing of the author, I can at best *infer* certain character traits as being the best explanation of certain recurrent themes, etc. in his work. Similarly, unless I already "know" that there is a God whose perfection is simply being, I cannot see his reality in the value my children have in just existing. In sum, the only kind of experience of God allowed by Aquinas' account is not an appropriate basis for asserting his existence. (In chapter 5 I will argue that there are veridical experiences of God in the sense of a good and powerful being who loves us; but God conceived in this way is very different from the transcendent Being Aquinas is discussing.)

(3) Can we, then, as the above analogy suggests, at least infer God's existence from what we know of the finite world? This possibility requires careful examination in view of Aquinas' own apparent belief that this could be done. It might seem that speaking of God as the cause of finite things is a basic mistake, since causal interaction takes place only between entities that can be described in terms of shared conceptual categories. Thus, when we

explain deviations from the expected orbit of Neptune by positing Pluto as their cause, this explanation is possible only because both Neptune and Pluto are gravitational masses, subject to the Newtonian laws of motion and gravitation. Without a common conceptualization of cause and effect, we cannot understand *how* the cause produces its effect, and so can give no content to the claim that there is a causal relation. (This, of course, is the root of the Cartesian problem of mind-body interaction.) Now since there is no possibility of a common conceptualization of God and creatures, it would seem that he cannot be their cause. (A Humean analysis of causality rejects the idea that we need to know how a cause produces its effect, on the grounds that there is no relation of production, only an observed constant conjunction inducing an expectation of its continuance. But such an analysis immediately excludes talk of God as cause of the universe because of the uniqueness and unobservability of both God and the universe.)

If it is a mistake even to talk of God as cause of the universe, then Aquinas' entire development of a language about God is incoherent because it starts from the nominal definition of God as "first cause of all things." However, the above argument applies only to one type of causal explanation (what Sellars calls the "interventionist" model of causality). There are other sorts of causal explanation that do not presuppose a common conceptualization of cause and effect. One instance is scientific explanation via the postulation of theoretical entities; for example, the explanation of the results of linear accelerator experiments by postulating elmentary particles. There are no descriptive terms (not even such basic ones as "spatial" and "temporal") applicable in the same sense to such particles and the objects whose behavior they are postulated to explain. This is the source of our puzzlement as to just how these two sorts of entities are related. (Are elementary particles somehow "part" of macro-objects? Are they "identical" with them? Do the two exist on different "levels"?) But

the lack of a common conceptualization and our conse-
quent puzzlement about the nature of the causal relation
does not affect the appropriateness of postulating the reality of the elementary particles that explain what we ob-
serve. Similarly, the uniqueness of God's nature does not
exclude the possibility of our speaking of him as the cause
of creatures.

But the question remains, Could there be evidence justifying the postulation of God as the cause of creatures?
Or, equivalently, could there be features of the world as
we know it that require a divine explanation? Here there
are two possibilities. The first is that there are *specific* features of the universe that require God as their explanation.
This is what is claimed by traditional arguments from miracles; that is, from the occurrence of extraordinary events
that can be plausibly explained only as the results of divine
action. It is sometimes said that a miracle in this sense
would have to be a "violation of the laws of nature"; that
is, the occurrence of an event inconsistent with some true
causal generalization about the world. If so, the argument
from miracles is on very shaky ground, because (as we
noted in chapter 1) laws of nature will be consistent with
any observable course of nature. Finding out that one had
been violated would require establishing that there were no
factors (not even ones entirely unknown to present science)
affecting the way the events governed by the law developed. But if the existence of such factors were excluded,
surely it would be at least as reasonable to suppose that
the purported law of nature was erroneous as it would be
to suppose that a true law of nature had been violated by
divine action. So it is hard to see how there could ever be
convincing evidence that a miracle in the sense of a violation of a law of nature had occurred.

Perhaps, however, a miracle (an event requiring explanation by reference to God) need not be a violation of a law
of nature. After all, God is in some sense a person and so
to say that he is the explanation of a given event is to say

that the event must be understood as the action of a personal agent. But the mere existence of a scientific explanation for an event does not exclude an explanation of it in terms of personal agency. Thus, there may be a complete scientific explanation for the vanishing of the picture on a television set in terms of optical stimuli that trigger certain brain events that cause muscular contractions that cause the movement of a knob, and so forth. But this is entirely consistent with the fact that the picture disappeared because I turned the set off. (This point, incidentally, is independent of any views we might have about freedom, though only compatibilism allows for the simultaneous possibility of a *complete* scientific explanation and an explanation in terms of *free* actions.) This suggests that we might be able to find events quite in accord with laws of nature but nonetheless needing explanation by the divine agent. But why would such an event, no matter how much power or wisdom it manifested, be more plausibly attributed to "the first cause of all things" rather than to a less ultimate agent of magnificient qualities? Further, why should we prefer to explain such an event by anything other than the ordinary interventionist mode of causality? Miracles in the sense that does not connote violation of natural laws might be a basis of arguing for the existence of some sort of superhuman being but not for the existence of God as Aquinas has characterized him. On the other hand, the existence of the "first cause of all things" might be distinctively manifested by a violation of a law of nature (the thought being that only the ordainer of such laws could suspend them); but, as we have seen, there are in principle epistemic obstacles to identifying the occurrence of miracles in this sense.

The second possibility of a causal argument for God's existence is one that starts from *global* rather than specific features of the universe; for example, its overall design or the mere fact that a universe exists at all. It is here, if at all, that Aquinas' account of God-talk allows for a justification of religious belief. Traditional interpretations of Aquinas have, of course, taken the five ways as deductive arguments for the existence of God. Specifically, each argument is seen as showing the need to posit God as the first in some global order of causality. But such a construal of the five ways is excluded by Burrell's interpretation of Aquinas' account of God-talk. Consider, for example, the first way, which purports to prove the existence of God as the first member of the series of movers producing any particular motion. It is clear that the first mover concluded to by this argument cannot be God as Aquinas subsequently characterizes him. As a member of a series of movers, the first mover would have to cause motion in the same sense that the other members of the series do. For the ultimate effect of motion produced by the last mover in a series is the same as the effect that would have been produced by the first mover acting alone on the object ultimately moved. So the concept 'mover' applies to the first mover in the same sense that it applies to the other movers. Since, on Burrell's interpretation, no concept can be applied in the same sense to God and creatures, God cannot be the first mover. Similarly, the other ways, taken as deductive arguments, rest on an illegitimate inclusion of God under creaturely categories. The second makes him an efficient cause, the fifth a final cause. The fourth presents him as a maximal instance of creaturely perfections. And the third way places God under the category of contingency by asserting that he is noncontingent. (Also, this way claims that God is necessary in a sense in which even creatures — e.g., angels — can be necessary.)[6]

So, on Burrell's interpretation, the standard deductive justifications that Aquinas might give for God's existence are ruled out in principle. Is there nonetheless room for some other sort of justification? To see that there is, we need to reflect on the logic of explanation involved in attempts to establish God's existence on the basis of global features of the universe. There is no doubt that there are

some such global features (e.g., the universe does exist) or
that, if there is need for a special explanation of such features, only God (as first cause) can provide it. The question is whether such features in fact need to be explained.
Typically, proponents of teleological or cosmological arguments urge that consistency requires us to make the
same explanatory demands for "global facts" as we do for
more specific facts; and critics urge that demands for explanations are misplaced for the case of "global facts." It
seems to me this dispute has remained unresolved because
both sides have failed to understand the nature of the explanatory demands they are arguing about. Proponents see
that it is legitimate to ask for an explanation of any fact
and from this conclude that there must always *be* an explanation. Critics see that we have no right to presuppose
that an explanation exists for every fact and from this conclude that it is not legitimate to ask for an explanation of
just any fact. Both sides see important truths but draw incorrect inferences from them. This is because they both
assume that the demand for an explanation involves the
assumption that an explanation exists.

To resolve the dispute, we need to realize that this is a
false assumption, that our explanatory demands should
not be construed as ontological presuppositions but as
methodological injunctions. It is always appropriate to
look for an explanation, but there is no guarantee that we
shall find one. From this standpoint, it is apparent that
traditional cosmological and teleological arguments fail
because they gratuitously assume that there must be an
explanation of the existence of the universe, etc.[7] On the
other hand, traditional criticisms of such arguments miss
the mark to the extent that they assume that there is no
point to seeking such explanations (at least until there is
some assurance that one can be found). It is as if half the
scientific community claimed it was *a priori* certain that
atoms were composed of more basic particles in terms of
which we can explain atomic behavior, and the other half

claimed that there was no point pursuing such a hypothesis. Obviously, both sides to such a controversy would be wrong, and the correct view would be one that urged development of accounts of subatomic particles but withheld judgment on the reality of such particles until we saw how fruitful and illuminating these accounts proved to be. Similarly, I suggest that, although a decision about the existence of God as the explanation of the existence or overall order of the universe cannot be made *a priori,* it can and should be made by assessing the extent to which developing such an explanation proves fruitful and illuminating.

The sort of assessment I have in mind will hinge on two primary considerations. The first is the extent to which thinking of the world as God's creation leads us to new truths about it. This kind of support for theism is well illustrated by Burrell's examples of ways in which Aquinas' development of a language about God might lead us to experience new dimensions of finite reality. The second consideration is the extent to which a developed theistic account of the world explains and thereby unites and completes our other general accounts (e.g., scientific, philosophical, moral) of things. This is not a matter of proving God's existence from scientific, or other, premises, or even of translating talk about God into the language of science, or any other language. It involves introducing talk of God as a *new* explanatory dimension, not as a postulation within the existing domain of discourse about creatures. Because of this, Aquinas' strictures about not speaking of God as we speak of creatures are not violated; but, at the same time, the appropriateness of such talk is justified by the new level of explanatory power it introduces. Although, given Burrell's interpretation, the five ways cannot be taken as deductive proofs, they can be regarded as justifications in the above sense.

Consider once again the first way. From our new perspective this can be viewed as an effective demonstration of how the Aristotelian world-system of bodies in motion can be explanatorily related to God. The idea is that, instead of merely asking why some particular motion occurs, we might ask why there is any motion at all. Asking such a question opens the way to positing the existence of God as the cause of motion. For such a cause would have to be unmoved (not in the sense of at rest but in the sense of being outside the categories of rest and motion); and, as a result, it would have to exercise its causality very differently from causes that produce motion by themselves moving (and so share with their effects the characterization "mobile"). Because God is beyond the categories of motion and rest, and because he produces effects with which he shares no common characterizations, it is consistent (though not necessary) to identify him as the cause of the very existence of motion. In a similar manner, the other four ways can be seen as asking for explanations of the existence of efficient causes, contingent beings, grades of perfection, and final causes; and, in each case, showing that God can be posited as the appropriate explanation.

It may seem that this use of the theistic arguments is a trivial exercise, merely a matter of asking for an explanation of some arbitrarily chosen fact and then positing God, who is after all defined as the cause of everything, as the explanation. But this is not so. First, the five ways do not make an arbitrary selection of facts to be explained. They select facts that correspond to basic categories of major explanatory systems of Aquinas' time. Thus, the first way deals with the motion that is the main object of Aristotelian astronomy and physics; the second with the system of efficient causes that Avicenna had distinguished from Aristotle's "moving causes"; the third with Aquinas' own basic metaphysical categories of necessary and contingent existence; the fourth with the Platonic-Augustinian notion of metaphysical perfection; and the fifth with the pervasively employed concept of final causality. Second, it is not true that God can be properly introduced as the explanation of just any fact. He is the first cause of all things, but not all explanatory demands are appropriately met by an appeal to the first cause. Reference to God is appropriate only when giving an explanation requires postulating a cause characterized by the same predicates with which we characterize God (which does not mean that the predicates must apply to the cause in the same way that they do to God). Thus, explaining the very existence of motion requires a cause that is in some sense unmoved. By contrast, an explanation of the fact that gases expand when heated or that humans sometimes perform evil actions would not require reference to a cause characterized by the predicates we ascribe to God. The motions of molecules and the weakness of human wills would be sufficient explanations.

Thus the achievement of the five ways (if they are successful) is by no means trivial. They show that the fundamental explanatory categories of a wide range of medieval modes of thinking about the world can all themselves be explained by reference to God. Accordingly, raising the explanatory questions that lead to a positing of God effects a major unification of our efforts to understand reality. Further, Aquinas' work shows that his view of the world as God's creation has consequences for almost every major philosophical question, from the status of universals to the nature of morality. When these systematic virtues of God-talk are combined with the increased riches it brings to our experience of the world, we have significant support for including God in our account of reality.

It is apparent, then, that Aquinas' claim that God exists is open to justification on the basis of both its ability to lead us to new truths and its explanatory power. This is not to say that Aquinas intended to carry out a justification of this sort. Nor is it to say that a similar justification could be successfully carried out in today's very different intellectual context. Judgments of each of these questions would require extensive treatments in their own right. But for our purposes the crucial point is that, even given Burrell's interpretation of Aquinas on God-talk, the proposition 'God exists' is open to justifications. Admittedly, the sort of justification that is relevant is not a *proof* in the ordinary sense of a single line of deductive or inductive argument in which universally accepted rules of inference applied to incontestable premises yield a logically impeccable conclusion. The relevant model of justification is much more like Newman's idea of several different lines of thought that converge to an informed and rational (but by no means inevitable) judgment. There is no doubt that this sort of justification by "judgment" rather than "proof" is a legitimate way of drawing conclusions that plays a central role in many areas of human life. Indeed, I think that a strong case can be made for the view that it represents the primary mode of justification in *every* area. Certainly, recent work on the nature of scientific rationality – especially that of Kuhn and Toulmin – has supported the conclusion that scientific justification fits the "judgment" rather than the "proof" model. In chapter 4 we shall assess the effectiveness of this approach, in the context of present-day thought, as a justification of religious belief. In any case, it is clear that there are considerations relevant to the truth or falsity of Aquinas' claim that God exists, and so it cannot be properly taken as a Wittgensteinian "groundless belief."

Of course the fact that the Wittgensteinian thesis turns out to be inconsistent with one interpretation of Aquinas' account of religious language does not prove the thesis false. There may be other accounts of religious language, far superior to the one we have discussed, that support the thesis. Certainly, nothing I am arguing for requires an *acceptance* of the Aquinas-Burrell account. My point is rather that this account seems to go as far as possible, short of an obviously unacceptable internalism, toward the sort of uniqueness of religious language that is needed to support the Wittgensteinian thesis. Its failure to support the thesis raises serious questions as to whether Wittgensteinians could find any adequate account of religious language that would support their views. Moreover, it seems likely that a role for justification would enter into any noninternalist account of religious langauge in much the way that it entered into the Aquinas-Burrell account. Any talk of God that would make a difference to us would have to lead to our awareness of new sorts of truths or at least cohere with our other accounts of reality. Otherwise, it will be no more than an isolated, purely formal, game. But talk of God that is not thus isolated would seem to be open to justification by the methods we illustrated for Aquinas' case.

In conclusion, let me suggest, without developing the point as it deserves, that the Wittgensteinian approach fails because, in spite of its frequent perceptiveness, it ultimately misrepresents the nature of religion. For the Wittgensteinian, religion is a form of life; that is, a system of beliefs that, on the most fundamental level, constitute a way of leading a human life. Though this might seem an entirely appropriate view, given the depth and power of religious commitments, I believe it distorts the role of the great world religions, which define our primary religious options. Such religions do not constitute our basic forms of life but rather criticize and transform them. Primitive religions, like that of the Zande, may be inextricable elements of their society and so perhaps cannot be evaluated by those within that society. But such religions are entirely *naturalistic* in the sense that they represent no truths or values beyond those fundamental for the society in which they function. By contrast, Christianity, Buddhism, Hinduism, etc. articulate systems of truths and values designed to challenge and transform their societies. Of course, they call us to new "forms of life" in some sense, but this is a matter of *reform* within a way of life that is presupposed by the religious call for reform and that in essential ways continues to underlie the life of one who answers the call and believes. Our religions speak to the human condition as it is already constituted by fundamental forms of life. As we put it above, they provide answers to questions that arise prior to them; and the answers provided would not be answers to these questions if they required the abandonment of the forms of life that generate the questions.

The point can be driven home by reflecting on the difference between those of us who hold religious beliefs and members of primitive tribes. If Winch's account is correct, there is no way of being an Azande without believing in witchcraft and poison-oracles. So no one born into the Zande form of life can give up such beliefs without becoming an outsider to Zande society — for example, by becoming westernized or going mad. But a twentieth-century American given the most devout and pervasive religious upbringing does not become an outsider to American society by ceasing to believe in God. The American has not abandoned a form of life but rather a way of thinking and acting *within* a form of life. This is because for us religion exists not as a form of life but as a challenge and option within our form of life. And this is why even the most committed believers must, as their religion itself will insist, see nonbelief as a real possibility for them. Because our religions define themselves within and in relation to our forms of life, it is inevitable that their claims will fall within the scope of the methods of justification characteristic of these forms of life.

Thus, for us, religion is neither naturalistic (woven into the very fabric of our form of life) nor transcendent (a call to an entirely new form of life). If it were either or these, belief might well be properly groundless. But then it would lose its distinctive and invaluable character as a call to transform — without renouncing — our human condition.

3. Disagreement and the Need for Justification

1. Plantinga's Claim that 'God Exists' Is Properly Basic

Our reflections on Wittgensteinian approaches to religion have led to the conclusion that believers cannot avoid demands for justification by appealing to some special epistemic role for their fundamental beliefs, a role that would make the project of justifying them ultimately unintelligible. But there is another possibility. Believers might maintain that, although their beliefs are entirely open to justification (and perhaps have been or will someday be justified), their right to believe does not depend on carrying out any justification. Here there are some apparently parallel cases: All of us believe that material objects exist when none of us perceive them, that other people have an inner conscious life like ours, that there are regularities observed in the past that will hold in the future. Philosophers dispute how or whether such claims can be justified. Some propose methods of justification, others (along Wittgensteinian lines) urge that the question of justification cannot be properly raised. But, beyond these disputes, two things remain certain: (1) Most people have neither justified these claims nor shown that demands for their justificaiton are inappropriate; (2) we are all nonetheless entitled to believe these claims. This shows that the possibility mentioned above has some actual instances. There are cases where we are entitled to believe without justification but have no reason for thinking that the question of justification is inappropriate. Can religion be rightly regarded as another such instance?

Alvin Plantinga has recently defended an affirmative response to the question.[1] He discusses the demand for a justification of religious belief as it arises in the context of a foundationalist view of knowledge.[2] Accordingly, his first task is to characterize with some precision the foundationalist viewpoint. He begins by introducing the notion of a person's *noetic structure*; i.e., "the set of propositions he believes together with certain epistemic relations that hold among him and these propositions" ("The Reformed Objection to Natural Theology," p. 54). The most important of these relations is *being-a-basis-of-belief-in*. Thus, I typically believe some propositions (e.g., that apricot jam is an ingredient of a Sacher Torte) on the basis of other propositions (e.g., that the *Viennese Pastry Cookbook* lists it as an ignredient or that the Sacher Torte served at Demel's contains apricot jam). A belief may, however, be held without the basis of any other belief. This is typically true of the belief that 2+1=3 or that I am feeling pain. Such beliefs are *basic* within a person's noetic structure. The set of all the basic beliefs of a noetic structure is its *foundation*.

Foundationalism for Plantinga is a normative thesis about the nature of *rational* noetic structures. Specifically, *weak foundationalism* involves two claims: (1) "Every rational noetic structure has a foundation"; that is, there is a set of basic propositions on the basis of which all other propositions of a rational noetic structure are believed. (2) "In a rational noetic structure, non-basic belief is proportional in strength to support from the foundation" (p. 56). Weak foundationalism is very plausible and widely accepted even by philosophers (e.g., Sellars, Quine) who are in other ways antifoundationalist; and Plantinga himself seems inclined to endorse it.[3] If we add to weak foundationalism a set of criteria claimed to define the set of permissible basic propositions, we have *strong foundationalism.* Given weak foundationalism, strong foundationalism seems a necessary further step, because without criteria for what may be taken as basic there could be rational noetic structures that took almost any absurd set of beliefs as basic. Historically, however, strong foundationalism has most often been formulated in terms of three specific criteria. *Self-evidence* and *incorrigibility* are the criteria of basicality employed by Cartesian philosophers; ancient and medieval philosophers (e.g., Aristotle and Aquinas) have also allowed as basic those propositions that are *evident to the senses* (the immediate deliverances of sense perception). Plantinga labels *classical foundationalism* the view that any properly basic proposition must be self-evident, incorrigible, or evident to the sense. Classical foundationalism requires a justification of religious beliefs (because they have none of the three features sufficient for basicality). But Plantinga thinks it is an untenable view,[4] and his position is surely supported by the arguments of many contemporary antifoundationalists.

Plantinga holds, then, that we may properly take as basic those propositions that are neither self-evident nor incorrigible nor evident to the sense. He does not, however, hold that anyone can properly take just anything as basic. He allows that some propositions (e.g., 'the Great Pumpkin returns every Halloween') cannot be properly basic and that propositions that are properly basic under some conditions are not properly basic under others (e.g., 'there is a tree in my yard' can be properly taken as basic if I am directly looking at the tree but not if I am listening to music with my eyes closed). There are criteria, other than those of classical foundationalism, that exclude some propositions from the foundations of a rational noetic structure.

At this point, a critic may object that Plantinga still needs to provide the criteria of proper basicality that allow belief in God but exclude belief in the Great Pumpkin and other absurdities. To this Plantinga offers the following response:

> This objection betrays an important misconception. How *do* we rightly arrive at or develop criteria for . . . proper basicality? Where do they come from? Must one have such a criterion before one can sensibly make any judgments — positive or negative — about proper basicality? Surely not. Suppose I don't know of a satisfactory substitute for the criteria proposed by classical foundationalism; I am nevertheless entirely within my rights in holding that certain propositions are not properly basic in certain conditions [p. 59].

Further, Plantinga argues, the only way to develop nontrivial criteria of proper basicality is on the basis of examples:

> The fact is, I think that [no] necessary and sufficient condition for proper basicality follows from obviously self-evident premises by obviously acceptable arguments. And hence the proper way to arrive at such a criterion is, broadly speaking, *inductive*. We must assemble examples of beliefs and conditions such that the former are obviously properly basic in the latter, and examples of beliefs and conditions such that the former are obviously not properly basic in the latter. We must then frame hypotheses as to the necessary and sufficient conditions of proper basicality and test these hypotheses by reference to those examples [p. 60].

But, he goes on to say in a crucial passage, the examples that we take as obvious in our development of criteria of basicality need not be shared by everyone:

> . . . there is no reason to assume, in advance, that everyone will agree on the examples. The Christian will of course suppose that belief in God is entirely proper and rational; if he doesn't accept

this belief on the basis of other propositions, he will conclude that it is basic for him and quite properly so. Followers of Bertrand Russell and Madelyn Murray O'Hare may disagree; but how is that relevant? Must my criteria, or those of the Christian community, conform to their examples? Surely not. The Christian community is responsible to *its* set of examples, not to theirs [pp. 60–61].

In sum, then, Plantinga's defense of the claim that 'God exists' may be properly basic for the Christian is as follows: there are no obviously correct criteria for proper basicality; therefore, we must develop such criteria inductively on the basis of obvious examples (clear cases) of properly basic propositions. For the Christian (at least one whose belief in God does not rest on inferences from other propositions) 'God exists' is one of these obvious examples.

What seems to me most problematic here is Plantinga's assumption that disagreement about the epistemic status of 'God exists' has no relevance to the propriety of taking it as an obvious example of proper basicality. He is saying not only that, for the Christian, so disputed a proposition as 'God exists' is properly basic but also that its proper basicality is obvious and so in no need of support from criteria of proper basicality. Now it is surely true that the mere fact of some disagreement about a proposition need not lead us to question its truth or proper basicality. I can, for example, rightly disregard the dissent of the lunatic or the eccentric philosopher who thinks that he or she is the only person in the world. But the disagreement of substantial numbers of those who, as far as I can tell, are my *epistemic peers* (i.e., my equals in intelligence, perspicacity, honesty, thoroughness, and other relevant epistemic virtues) is surely another matter. Isn't it just common sense to admit that, when there is widespread agreement about a claim, with apparently competent judges on both sides, those who assert or deny the claim need to justify their positions?

It might be suggested that, appearances to the contrary, religious believers have no epistemic peers who disagree with them. Perhaps those who do not see 'God exists' as obviously basic have minds clouded by the effects of sin and so are not the epistemic equals in this matter of those whose minds have been illuminated by divine grace. Plantinga in fact seems inclined to a view of this sort put forward by John Calvin:

> Calvin's claim, then, is that God has created us in such a way that we have a strong propensity or inclination towards belief in him. This tendency has been in part overlaid or suppressed by sin. Were it not for the existence of sin in the world, human beings would believe in God to the same degree and with the same natural spontaneity that we believe in the existence of other persons, an external world, or the past. This is the natural human condition; it is because of our presently unnatural sinful condition that many of us find belief in God difficult or absurd. The fact is, Calvin thinks, one who doesn't believe in God is in an epistemically substandard position — rather like a person who doesn't believe that his wife exists, or thinks she is like a cleverly constructed robot and has no thoughts, feelings or consciousness [pp. 51–52].

There are, however, deep difficulties with invoking such a view in the present context. One is that the view itself derives from theological doctrines that presuppose theism and so cannot be legitimately called upon in a defense of the believer's epistemic right to accept theism. Another is that there are at least some believers who themselves do not see 'God exists' as obviously properly basic; it is very hard to see how the believer can nonarbitrarily apply Calvin's view to deny that they are his epistemic peers.

So we must proceed on the assumption that believers do have epistemic peers who disagree with their assessment that 'God exists' is properly basic. The question is whether this disagreement should lead believers to withdraw their claim that 'God exists' is for them a clear case of a properly basic proposition and (supposing they have no reason for believing 'God exists' beyond its alleged proper basicality) their claim that God exists. More fully, there is, on the one hand, the view that, all else being equal, the fact of disagreement about religious beliefs poses a challenge to those beliefs. Because there are those, seemingly as qualified as the believer to judge the matter, who do not believe, we must conclude that believers must either justify their belief by argument or else show it to have some special status that puts it beyond justification. On the other hand, common sense often judges that, when there is disagreement that has not been resolvable by argument (e.g., about the existence of extraterrestrial intelligences), everyone is entitled to his or her own opinion, even in matters where there is in principle no obstacle to a justification of one of the opposing views. So if, after an honest but inconclusive pursuit of arguments on both sides of the issue, it still seems to believers that their belief is correct, why should they not be entitled to it?

To approach this question let us consider the case of disagreement among epistemic peers in another context. Suppose a mathematician has reflected long and hard on a given proposition (e.g., the axiom of choice) and, although he is not able to derive it as a theorem or even to put forward strong plausibility arguments for it, has come to an entirely firm conviction of its truth. He just "sees" that it is true. However, when he proposes his proposition to his equally competent colleagues, he meets mixed reactions. Some share his intuitive acceptance of the proposition, others do not. In such a case, is he entitled to continue believing the proposition or should he withhold judgment on it?

Suppose that whenever the mathematician encounters the disagreement of a colleague he does no more than note it and reassert his own commitment. He arbitrarily refuses to discuss the disagreement and does not listen to any considerations his colleague might put forward in opposition to his view. Surely in such a case we must say that the mathematician is being irrational and that he has no right to continue holding his belief. To be entitled to maintain his view, he must take account of his opponents' views in at least two ways: first, he must see whether they have any good arguments against his view; second, assuming that he concludes they do not, he must see if there is any reason to trust his opponents' judgment (intuition) rather than his own on this point. (Perhaps his opponents are more familiar with the relevant area of mathematics or have a better past record in having their intuitive judgments borne out.) We must, therefore, assume that our mathematician has considered carefully both these points and concluded that his opponents have no good arguments for their view and are not in a better position than he to judge the matter. In such a circumstance, is he still entitled to believe the proposition? Putting the issue more generally: If (1) there is no argument or evidence that entitles me to believe p and (2) p nonetheless seems to me obviously true but (3) there is equal division among my epistemic peers as to the obvious truth of p, then am I epistemically entitled to believe p?

One reason for thinking I am entitled to believe p in this situation might be that p's seeming obvious to me counts in favor of its truth. To see if this might be so we need to distinguish two importantly different cases: one in which those epistemic peers who dissent from my view see p as obviously false and one in which they merely do not see p as obviously true. In the former case, there are two relevant considerations. First, believing p is arbitrary in the sense that there is no reason to think that my intuition (i.e., what seems obviously true to me) is more likely to be correct than that of those who disagree with me. Believing p because its truth is supported by *my* intuition is thus an *epistemological egoism* just as arbitrary and unjustifiable as ethical egoism is generally regarded to be. This point can be driven home by considering another situation that is epistemically equivalent to that of the disagreement in the intuitions of peers. Suppose I find that on every other day it seems entirely clear to me that p is true, but that on the remaining days it seems entirely clear to me that p is false. Suppose further that there is no reason to think that my competence as a judge of p varies from day to day. Surely in such a situation I should not believe p, even on those days when it seems entirely clear to me. And the reason is that there is no basis for preferring my judgment on one day to my judgment on another. But surely there is no epistemically relevant difference between my judgments on different days and the judgments my epistemic peers and I make simultaneously.

A second consideration arises if we assess the situation from the standpoint of a neutral epistemic observer; that is, an observer who is as fully informed about the situation as I and my epistemic peers but who is not personally involved in any way that might improperly affect his judgment. In particular, the neutral epistemic observer has no intuitions pro or con about p and has not thought about p to an extent sufficient to make his not having any intuitions significant. From the point of view of such an observer, the facts are simply these (taking for simplicity the case of disagreement between two peers): (1) person A has an intuition that p is true; (2) person B has an intuition that p is false; (3) there is no reason to think that either A or B is more likely to be correct in his intuition. Surely the only proper attitude for such an observer is to withhold judgment on p. But even if I am A or B, should I not judge the situation in the same way as a neutral observer should? Surely it is wrong to prefer my intuition simply because it is mine.

But what of the case in which A has an intuition that p is true, and his epistemic peer B, rather than having an intuition of p's falsity, has, after careful reflection, no intuition at all about the truth or falsity of p? (This is closer to the case of religious belief, since nonbelievers do not typically insist on the obvious falsity of religion.) Here there are seemingly good arguments for both A's right to believe p and for A's obligation to withhold judgment. On the one hand, it may be argued that A's intuition provides support for believing p, whereas B's lack of an intuition provides equal support for not believing p (specifically, withholding judgment on it). Thus, we have a Jamesian situation of a forced option between alternatives that are equally acceptable from an epistemic viewpoint. Since A must prefer one of the alternatives, surely he has a right (if not an obligation) to chose the one that corresponds to his own intuition.

This line of thought can be further developed into an argument for the epistemic preferability of p. For, it might be claimed, the probability of p, given simply the fact of A's intuition, is very high — surely greater than 1/2; and the probability of p, given just B's lack of intuition, is exactly 1/2 (because, as far as B can see, p may just as well be true as false). Accordingly, it would seem that the probability of p, given *both* A's intuition *and* B's lack of it, will be the average of the two separate probabilities, and so greater than 1/2. Hence, it would seem to be more reasonable to believe p than not to believe it.

On the other hand, there is an attractive line of argument for the obligation to withhold judgment on p. A's experience provides evidence for believing that p is non-inferentially warranted, whereas B's experience provides equal, offsetting evidence for believing that p is not non-inferentially warranted. It is not, after all, just that B *happens* not to "see" the truth of p. B has looked carefully for it and is as competent as observer as A. So B's failure to "see" the truth of p suggests that this truth is not available to be seen (not that p is not true; just that its truth is not noninferentially warranted). So it would seem that there is nothing to chose between believing that p is non-inferentially warranted and believing that it is not. Consequently, we should withhold judgment on this question. Also, by hypothesis, the only basis we might have for believing p would be a belief that it is noninferentially warranted. So it follows that we should withhold judgment on *p*. And this applies even to A, if he wishes to be an epistemically responsible person.

As I see it, this latter argument is sound. What then is wrong with the argument for the opposite conclusion? In both its forms, this argument assumes that A's intuition supports belief in *p* independently of the fact that B has no similar intuition. That is, the argument not only (rightly) assumes that believing *p* is supported by the fact of A's intuition when this fact is the only evidence we have relevant to believing *p*; it also (wrongly) assumes that this support remains when we come to know of B's attitude toward *p*. This assumption is false for the following reason: A's intuition supports believing *p* only to the extent that it supports the claim that *p* is noninferentially warranted. The full line of thought here is: *p* seems noninferentially warranted to A; A is usually right about such matters; so *p* is probably noninferentially warranted. But, as the argument of the immediately preceding paragraph shows, when we add to the fact of A's intuition the fact of B's lack of such an intuition, support for the claim that *p* is noninferentially warranted disappears. The total relevant evidence does not support this claim. Accordingly, both forms of the argument for believing *p* are wrong in assuming that, when account is taken of the experiences of both A and B, the support for believing *p* is equal to or greater than the support for withholding judgment on *p*.

The essential point can be put this way: whenever I claim that a proposition is properly basic for me because I find it obviously true, I must claim that I am in an epistemic situation that gives me a privileged access to its truth. Thus, if 'there is a tree in my front yard' is basic for me, this is because I am in an epistemic situation (e.g., looking directly at the tree, with unimpaired eyesight, in clear sunlight) in which there is good reason to think that my noninferential judgment about the relevant topic (the tree) will be correct. If we can show that in fact there is no good reason to think that a person's epistemic situation provides a privileged access to the truth of a given proposition, then we have undermined the claim that the proposition is properly basic for that person. Thus, if someone claims that 'there is a tree in my front yard' is basic for him, that claim can be undermined by showing that there is no good reason to think that he is in a position to see the tree. Now one way of showing that there is no good reason to think that a person's epistemic situation provides a privileged access to the truth of a given proposition is to show that there are others in the same epistemic situation who do not have such access. Thus, if a trained microscope technician claims to see directly that a certain cell sample is cancerous, and another technician equally well trained and using the same equipment does not see this, then the first technician needs to offer further considerations, beyond his seeing that it is so, in support of the claim that the cells are cancerous. The thought is simply that the failure of an epistemic situation to provide privileged access to the truth of a proposition for some people raises doubt as to whether it provides such access for anyone.

Applying these considerations to religious belief, we seem led to the conclusion that, because believers have many epistemic peers who do not share their belief in God (and even more who do not share their belief that "God exists" is properly basic), they have no right to maintain their belief without a justification. If they do so, they are guilty of epistemological egoism.

This conclusion is, however, acceptable only with an important qualification. Throughout our discussion, we have limited ourselves to considerations relevant to the *truth* of propositions taken as properly basic. That is, we have assumed that when someone says a proposition is properly basic for him, he is claiming that there is something in his epistemic situation (e.g., his intuitions, the way he has been educated) that supports the truth of the proposition. Our case against epistemic egoism has been a matter of showing that, given the disagreement of peers, an individual's adherence to a proposition does not count decisively in favor of its truth.

But this qualification suggests a further possibility. Perhaps someone who claims that a proposition is properly basic for him need not claim that its being so says anything about the proposition's truth. Rather, he may merely claim that there are factors in his epistemic situation that entitle him to believe the proposition even though they do not support the proposition's truth. Here we can draw a useful parallel with propositions that require justification (i.e., propositions that are not properly basic). One method of justification is to give an argument that concludes that a given proposition is true: this is *truth-oriented* justification. But another method is to give an argument that concludes that it is appropriate or permissible to believe the proposition (on grounds other than its truth). Pragmatic arguments for religious belief and "vindications" of induction are of this sort. There can, of course, be no question of justifying a properly basic proposition, in any ordinary sense of "justification." Nonetheless, whenever a proposition is put forward as properly basic, there is still a need to give some account of the grounds of its proper basicality. Such an account may say that the proposition is self-evident in some technical sense, that it is impossible for me not to believe it, that it is utterly obvious, etc. If no account of any sort were required, anyone could rightly claim that any proposition is properly basic for him. So the fact that a proposition is said to be properly basic does not relieve us of the epistemic obligation to provide some sort of grounding for the proposition in our epistemic situation. (This of course does not mean that we are obliged to offer a generally applicable criterion of proper basicality.)

Returning to the question of religious beliefs, our discussion so far has concluded that there is nothing in the religious believer's epistemic situation that provides a truth-oriented ground for the proper basicality of his belief.

That is, there is nothing in the believer's epistemic situation (e.g., an intuition of self-evident truth) that grounds his belief's truth. But this does not exclude the possibility that the believer's epistemic situation provides a *truth-independent* ground for his right to believe. Specifically, we may ask why the believer cannot claim that the mere fact that he believes (or that what he believes seems obvious to him) is itself sufficient grounds for taking his belief as basic. It would, of course, be absurd to think that this sort of move will always be appropriate; for then anyone could rightly take all his beliefs as properly basic. But, as we have already noted, there is a common-sense inclination to say that, when there is unresolvable controversy about a question, everyone is entitled to his own belief. Along the same lines, some recent epistemological discussions have suggested that, in some circumstances, the mere fact that I believe a proposition can be an adequate ground for my right to believe the proposition. This suggestion has been formulated in a *principle of methodological conservatism.* In the following section, I will discuss this principle and the possibility of applying it to religious belief.

2. Religious Belief and Methodological Conservatism

My discussion of methodological conservatism will fall into three parts: (1) an examination of D. Goldstick's argument against methodological conservatism; (2) an examination of Larry Sklar's defense of it; (3) my own attempt to formulate a principle of methodological conservatism and to apply it to the justification of religious belief.[5]

(1) D. Goldstick[6] introduced the expression "methodological conservatism" to refer to the view held, in one way or another, by various philosophers (e.g., Hume, Quine, Chisholm), that "*a priori* and in principle, it is possible (at least sometimes) to make out a good *prima*

facie case for a proposition by citing the fact that it is believed by us" ("Methodological Conservatism," p. 186).
The distinctiveness of the principle of methodological conservatism lies in the qualification "*a priori* and in principle,"
which Goldstick takes to exclude the noncontroversial case
of appeal to an authority that has been proved reliable by
past experiences. The conservative idea is that the *mere*
fact that someone believes *p* (quite apart from any empirical information about the reliability of his belief) is a
reason in favor of his believing *p*. (Thus, Peirce's view, that
there are evolutionary reasons for thinking that the mere
fact that we are inclined to a belief is a point in favor of it,
is *not* an example of methodological conservatism.)

Although Goldstick allows that a principle of methodological conservatism may be valid for a few special cases
(e.g., the belief that I exist or that I am in pain), he thinks
there is a decisive argument against the general validity of
such a principle:

> It seems evident enough that, just as it is logically impossible for
> there to exist both a true belief and a true disbelief in the same
> proposition, so it is likewise logically impossible for there to exist
> both a justified belief and a justified disbelief in the very same
> proposition, given the same body of available facts. If the avail-
> able facts are such as to justify believing the proposition, they
> will not be such as to justify disbelieving it. If belief in a proposi-
> tion is no more justified than disbelief in it and disbelief in it no
> more justified than belief, neither belief nor disbelief is
> justified. . . .
>
> These considerations suggest an argument that can be brought
> against methodological conservatism — indeed, a decisive one, I
> think. A methodological conservative is obliged to hold with re-
> gard to any belief which he justifies holding on a basis of
> methodological conservatism, that someone with an opposite
> belief to his own would be equally justified in holding that op-
> posite belief even if neither of them were acquainted with any
> grounds for belief or disbelief with which the other one was not

acquainted also. This surely shows the position of methodological conservatism to be rationally untenable [pp. 186–87].

What exactly is Goldstick's argument here? It can best be understood by considering a situation specified by the following three conditions:

(1) Person A is justified in believing p.
(2) Person B is justified in believing not-p.
(3) A and B have exactly the same evidence (E) relevant to the belief in p and in not-p.

According to Goldstick, the situation specified by these conditions is logically impossible. But, he says, methodological conservatism entails that it is logically possible. Therefore, he concludes, methodological conservatism is false.

Let us try to see why Goldstick thinks the situation specified by (1)–(3) is logically impossible (i.e., why he thinks the three propositions entail a contradiction). On Goldstick's view, (1) is equivalent to:

(1′) A's evidence relevant to belief in p and in not-p justifies believing p.

And, similarly, (2) is equivalent to:

(2′) B's evidence relevant to belief in p and in not-p justifies believing p.

Because, according to (3), the evidence referred to in (1′) and (2′) is the same (namely, E), it follows that:

(4) E justifies believing p

and

(5) E justifies believing not-p.

Goldstick believes that (4) and (5) are mutually inconsistent: ". . . it is . . . logically impossible for there to exist both a justified belief and a justified disbelief in the very same proposition, given the same body of available facts" (p. 186). This conclusion follows from his understanding of justification. He says that, in the context of a discussion of methodological conservatism, "justification" means "epistemic justification" and that "for a belief to be 'epistemically justified' means that in the interests of truth it is best to hold it [in the existing circumstances]" (p. 186). Restating (4) and (5) in terms of this understanding of justification yields:

(4') Given E, in the interests of truth it is best to believe p

and

(5') Given E, in the interests of truth it is best to believe not-p.

If (4') and (5') were both true, then it would follow that, given E, it would be in the interest of truth best to believe p and not-p; that is, it would be in the interest of truth best to believe something that we know to be false. Because this is obviously absurd, (4') and (5') cannot both be true.

However, Goldstick's argument here depends on interpreting justification as an absolute relationship between a proposition and a body of evidence, quite independent of the persons who are aware of the evidence and believe the propositions. The idea of methodological conservatism is better represented by a view that relativizes justification to individuals. Thus, we might replace (4) and (5) with:

(4a) E justifies A's believing p

and

(5a) E justifies B's believing not-p.

This eliminates any contradiction between the two propositions.

It might be objected, however, that this is an illegitimate move. Recall that a belief is justified just in case it is, in the interests of truth, best to hold it. If it is in the interests of truth best for A to believe p, then surely it is in the interests of truth best for *anyone* in the same epistemic circumstances to believe p. For what it is best for A to believe is not a function of the "accident" of his being A but of the circumstances, relevant to making judgments about the truth or falsity of propositions, in which A finds himself. But B is in the same epistemic circumstances as A, because both have exactly the same body of evidence relevant to the truth or falsity of p. Therefore, if it is best for A to believe p, then it is also best for B to believe p.

This objection depends on the assumption that A and B are in the same epistemic circumstances. This is true in the sense that both have exactly the same evidence for the truth or falsity of p. But they are not in the same epistemic circumstances to the extent that A believes p and B believes not-p. Methodological conservatism asserts that what it is best for A or for B to believe depends not only on the evidence each of them has for the truth or falsity of p (which is the same) but also on what each of them in fact believes about p (which is different). So to assume that A and B are in the same epistemic circumstances relevant to p is simply to beg the question against methodological conservatism by assuming that what A and B in fact believe about p is not relevant to what it is best for them to believe about p.

These considerations have force if methodological conservatism is taken as a principle for what I have called *truth-independent* justification of beliefs. That is, if it is taken as suggesting that, in addition to evidence for the truth or falsity of a proposition, there may be considerations independent of the question of its truth or falsity relevant to the question of whether we are justified in believing it. This means that whether, in the interests of truth, it is best for a person to believe p may depend on more than the evidence the person has for p's truth or falsity. Goldstick's objection to methodological conservatism is sound only if we assume that support depends solely on evidence for truth and falsity. But methodological conservatism, as I propose to present it, is based on precisely the denial of this view.

(2) Larry Sklar[7] formulates a principle of methodological conservatism as follows:

> If you believe some proposition, on the basis of whatever positive warrant may accrue to it from the evidence, apriori plausibility, and so forth, it is unreasonable to cease to believe the proposition to be true merely because of the existence of, or knowledge of the existence of, alternative incompatible hypotheses whose positive warrant is no greater than that of the proposition already believed ["Methodological Conservatism," p. 378].

Sklar emphasizes that this formulation avoids the suggestion (implicit in Goldstick's formulation) that my believing *p* gives it some positive warrant. He finds this an entirely implausible suggestion and takes conservatism as merely the idea that learning of equally warranted alternatives does not entitle us to give up beliefs already held.

Sklar's main suggestion for a justification of methodological conservatism consists in a kind of "transcendental argument." The argument presents methodological conservatism as a necessary consequence of rejecting skepticism, given what Sklar calls a "local" view of justification. The skeptical challenge can be put as follows. For me to be entitled to a belief B, the following conditions must be met: (1) I must have a justification for B; (2) I must be entitled to every belief employed in the justification of B. According to the skeptic, applying condition (2) to the beliefs used in the justification of any one of my beliefs generates a regress of justifications that will either become circular or else never terminate. Since I am not entitled to believe a proposition on the basis of a circular or an incomplete justification, I am not entitled to any of my beliefs.

The classic response to this skeptical argument is to divide my beliefs into two sets: those justified by other beliefs and those that are self-justified (e.g., self-evident). This denies the skeptic's implicit assumption that all justification must be by appeal to other beliefs and thus eliminates the necessity of circularity or infinite regress in our justification of B. However, the recent epistemological trend has been away from the idea of self-justified beliefs and toward an acceptance of the skeptic's view that justification is always a matter of derivation from other beliefs. This, in effect, is what Sklar means by the view that all justification is "local." "All justification requires a body of unchallenged background belief" (p. 397). But given such a view, how are we to answer the skeptic? Clearly, we must claim that we are entitled to some of our beliefs even though they are unjustified. Of course, such a claim is not appropriate for all our unjustified beliefs — for example, for those whose negations are justified. So the question is which unjustified beliefs are we entitled to. Sklar suggests that methodological conservatism provides the appropriate answer: we are entitled (indeed, required) to maintain an unjustified belief when there is nothing against the belief other than the existence of equally warranted incompatible alternatives.

Now assuming that there is no reason to think methodological conservatism is false, it clearly provides a sufficient condition for an adequate reply to the skeptic. But we need to establish the claim that it provides a necessary condition — or at least that it is preferable to any other sufficient condition as a response. This claim, however, is false. The skeptic, after all, claims that we are entitled to *none* of our beliefs. So refuting him requires only showing that we are entitled to one of our beliefs, and this requires only showing that we are entitled to the unjustified beliefs employed in the justification of this belief. (More simply, we can refute the skeptic by showing that there is an unjustified belief to which we are entitled.) Surely there are many claims far short of methodological conservatism that will provide what is needed to refute the skeptic. For example, we can claim that we are entitled to believe claims that seem to us necessary truths and about which there is substantial agreement among competent judges. Or we can claim that we are entitled to believe propositions that are evident to our senses. Such claims: (1) entail the falsity of skepticism; (2) are at least as plausible as methdological conservatism; and (3) may be true even if methodological conservatism is false. So it's hard to see that methodological conservatism is necessary to refute skepticism.

Further, there are reasons to think that Sklar's formulation of methodological conservatism is false. Consider, for example, a case in which I believe a mathematical claim (e.g., the axiom of choice) only because I regard a particular proof of it as sound. If I then discover that the proof is not sound and thereby realize that I have no more warrant for the claim than for its denial, surely it is not unreasonable for me to give up my belief. More generally, there will be counterexamples to Sklar's principle for any cases in which my learning of equally warranted alternatives to p of itself decreases my warrant for p to the point where there is no positive basis for believing it.

It might seem that we could avoid these counterexamples by adding a clause to the principle saying that it applies only in cases in which our learning of equally warranted alternatives to p does not decrease (or does not decrease to some specified extent) our warrant for p. But this move faces its own difficulties. Consider first cases where W_p (the initial warrant for p) is greater than $1/2$. In such a case, the discovery of just one equally warranted alternative to p will reduce the warrant for p to $1/2$ or less; and surely it is not irrational to withhold judgment on a proposition with such warrant. It is only for $W_p \leqslant 1/2$ that the discovery of an equally warranted alternative need not decrease W_p. But if $W_p \leqslant 1/2$, it is not clear that I was warranted in believing p in the first place, and it is very odd to say that it is unreasonable to give up a belief for which I never have had sufficient warrant. Further, no matter how small the initial warrant for p, the discovery of a sufficient number of equally warranted alternatives will always require a decrease in W_p. So it seems that, if the principle is amended to avoid the counterexamples of the preceding paragraph, there will be no cases to which it is significantly applicable.

Another kind of counterexample to Sklar's principle is the following. Suppose I believe that an undergraduate has plagiarized a paper on the plausible grounds that this is the only explanation for the extremely high quality of the work. If I subsequently learn that there is another equally warranted explanation (e.g., if I learn of his uncommon brilliance from conversations with him), then it is surely absurd to say that it is irrational for me to give up my initial belief. Indeed, it would seem that I am morally obliged to give up this belief (and at least withhold judgment on the student); and it would be very strange to claim that morality ever *requires* being unreasonable.

(3) I think we can avoid the difficulties of Sklar's formulation by making two moves. First, we should give up the attempt to have the principle express an epistemic obligation (what we must do to avoid being unreasonable) and instead formulate it as a statement of what is epistemically permissible (epistemic entitlement). Second, we should eliminate the reference to equally warranted alternative hypotheses and instead speak only about the epistemic status of p itself (and its negation). Specifically, we can introduce a principle of methodological conservatism in the following way. Let us say that a proposition is *epistemically indeterminate* for a person A if and only if the evidence of which A is aware relevant to the truth or falsity of p does not entitle him to believe p and does not entitle him to believe not-p. Given this, we can state a principle of methodological conservatism as follows:

If A believes p and p is epistemically indeterminate for him, then he is entitled to believe p.[8]

This formulation is not falsified by the counterexample of giving up belief in a mathematical claim when I realize that a proof I thought was sound is not. For this example shows only that there is nothing irrational about giving up a belief that is epistemically indeterminate, not that it is rationally necessary to give up such a belief. Also, it avoids the counterexample about the plagiarized paper because all it says is that, from an epistemic viewpoint (i.e., in terms of what is best from the point of view of truth), I have a right to continue believing that the student copied the paper. This is entirely consistent with an admission that, in this sort of case, my epistemic right is overridden by a moral obligation.

I further think that it is possible to argue for the truth of methodological conservatism as I have formulated it. The germ of an argument can be found in the following considerations. For just about all of us, it is highly likely that our beliefs on most controversial subjects are based on such a low level of understanding and such scanty and inaccurate information that those who have made a thorough study of the subject could easily show that our reasons for what we believe are woefully inadequate. For myself, for example, this is obviously true of my beliefs about controversial issues in economics (Is capitalism better than socialism?), politics (Are most government officials dishonest?), and psychology (Is a Freudian approach to dreams basically sound?). Further, even if I investigated the issues with as much thoroughness as would be practicable for me, there is good reason to think that the reasons for belief yielded by such an investigation would be easy targets for experts in the relevant field. So I have very good reason to think that my beliefs on these subjects are epistemically indeterminate. But it seems foolish to say that I have no right to maintain my beliefs on these subjects. For this is to say that I must unburden myself of all the most interesting and important of my beliefs, including many of those that are central to my character and personality. And the strangeness of such a conclusion becomes even more evident when we extend it to *everyone*. Surely we do not want to be so skeptical as to say that (almost) all of us ought to give up (almost) all our most important and characteristic beliefs.

These considerations can be developed into two different arguments. One would point out that a life of successful action in the world requires a person to have beliefs about a wide range of basic but controversial issues. Those who would withhold judgment across the board will become either opportunistic vacillators or else mere onlookers. However, though this pragmatic line of argument may justify methodological conservatism as a prudential or a moral principle, it does not give it epistemic status. That is, it does not establish methodological conservatism as a principle relevant to our interest in attaining the truth. However, this can be established by another, "Millian," line of argument. Surely, it can be argued, the interest of truth would be far better served by the lively conflict of firmly held beliefs than it would be by a general withdrawal from commitment on controversial issues. This is not to say that there is an epistemic duty, incumbent on everyone, to maintain epistemically indeterminate beliefs to which they are strongly inclined; the interest of truth is also greatly served by uncommitted inquirers. So the best policy in the interests of truth is to allow, but not require, those who believe a proposition (or, at least those who believe the proposition with a certain significant degree of conviction) to believe it even though it is epistemically indeterminate for them.

The validity of a principle of methodological conservatism offers a way of showing that the mere fact that I hold a belief provides a justification for holding the belief. Given our defense of the principle, such a justification will be truth-independent; that is, what will be justified is not the truth of the belief but the act of holding the belief. Before seeing how the principle might be applied to religious belief, it will be useful to make two clarificatory points about truth-independent justification.

(1) There is a *prima facie* oddity in the idea of justifying my act of believing (as opposed to the truth of my belief), since this seems to imply that my act of believing is an action (something I do), whereas in fact it is not an action but only an act in the minimal sense of an event or a

disposition. (To see this, suppose someone offers you the fondest desire of your heart if only you will, in the next five seconds, believe that you are on the moon; reflection on the fact that you cannot *do* this shows that it is not the sort of thing that can be done — i.e., not an action.) But it is actions, not events, that have reasons and hence justifications. So what is the sense of trying to justify a belief? Strictly speaking, there is no sense. But there is sense to engaging in a line of *action* that will initiate (or continue) acts of belief (or dispositions to such acts). So strictly we should speak of justifying the action of initiating or maintaining belief. But for convenience I will continue to speak loosely.

(2) There is no difference between believing a claim and believing that it is true. When I believe *p*, what I believe is precisely that *p* is true. So a truth-independent justification of religious belief must give good reason for believing that the claims of religion are true, not just for "accepting" them in the sense of living "in accord with" them, acting as if they were true. There may well be justifications for this sort of acceptance of religion, but such acceptance is a far cry from believers' traditional construal of their faith. It might seem that this insistence on the need to justify believing that religious claims are true cuts the ground from under any truth-independent justification. For doesn't a reason for believing that *p* is true come to the same thing as a reason for the truth of *p*? No. There is a distinction — and truth-independent justifications depend on it — between (a) reasons for the truth of *p* and (b) reasons for believing the truth of *p*. The reasons in (a) are expressed in propositions that stand in a relation of epistemic support to *p*; the reasons in (b) stand in a relation of epistemic support to 'I ought (or, I have a right) to believe *p*'.

These things said, let us ask what relevance the principle of methodological conservatism has to the justification of religious belief. In many ways, it seems to be highly relevant. First of all, it corresponds very closely to the attitude of many believers (including many of the most reflective) who admit that they can provide no positive arguments for their belief and yet maintain it on the grounds that there are no ultimately cogent objections to it. Further, the justification of religious belief by an appeal to methodological conservatism seems to have a number of important merits in comparison with other approaches.

(1) Unlike many contemporary critiques (and even some defenses) of religious belief, it presents the religious believer as a responsible rational agent. I count this an advantage on the same general grounds that philosophers of science, such as Lakatos, have regarded as suspect accounts of science that force us to regard the greater part of historical science as irrational. Just as philosophy of science should start from the methodological assumption that the bulk of science is rational, so too a philosophical analysis of any other reflective activity central in the history of the human race should assume that the activity is not pervaded with irrationality. This is not to say that an account is suspect simply because it is *skeptical* of religious claims. The methodological assumption I am invoking does not require that those making religious claims (any more than those making scientific claims) should be *right*: but it does require that most of them not be *benighted* – e.g., talking nonsense, asserting blatant non sequiturs, in the grip of a neurotic illusion.

(2) Unlike many contemporary defenses of religious belief, this approach does not radically transform the traditional meaning of religious assertions. It provides a way of justifying beliefs in their full-blooded, traditional sense. Thus, our justifications do not require interpreting "God is love" as "love is a central human value," or "Christ is God" as "the gospel account of Christ's life provides the highest moral ideal."

(3) Unlike many traditional apologetic efforts (especially in the Catholic tradition), this approach preserves the irreducible distinction (felt so deeply by many believers)

of faith from any form of nonreligious *knowledge.* Religious belief — though justified — does not become a species of historical, philosophical or experiential knowledge.

(4) Nonetheless, unlike many Wittgensteinian strategies, this approach does not appeal to any special notion of rationality, defensible only in terms of the conceptual framework or language-game of religious belief itself. Rather, the justification is based on values and principles that can be analyzed and defended quite independent of the religious viewpoint.

In spite of these merits, I think there is a fundamental difficulty with applying methodological conservatism to religious belief. This difficulty concerns the sort of assent to a belief authorized by methodological conservatism. Although numerous forms of assent can be distinguished, the two that are crucial for our purposes are what I will call *decisive assent* and *interim assent.* Decisive assent to p is defined by the fact that it terminates the process of inquiry into the truth of p. This does not mean that I no longer think about p, but my thoughts are concerned with developing its significance (analyzing its meaning, determining its implications) rather than establishing its truth. Nor does it mean that I am unconditionally committed to p; i.e., that I intend to maintain p no matter what evidence subsequently presents itself. Rather it means that I view the present case for p as allowing me to end the *search* for reasons for or against believing p. Interim assent, on the other hand, accepts p but without terminating inquiry into the truth of p. Its effect is to put me on the side of p in disputes about its truth. However, my endorsement of p is combined with a commitment to the epistemic need for continuing discussions of p's truth. (Someone who decisively assents to p may of course take part in discussions of p's truth and even think that such discussions are needed — e.g., to lead others to believe p — but he does not think that these discussions are epistemically necessary; that is, necessary for the project of determining the truth.)

Given this distinction of types of assent, I want to make the following claims. (1) When believing *p* is authorized by methodological conservatism, this is so only in the sense of interim assent. (2) Religious belief requires decisive, not just interim, assent. The first claim follows directly from the sort of epistemic justification we have been able to provide for methodological conservatism. I am entitled to believe *p* because doing so is likely to contribute to effecting a discussion with a maximal chance of arriving at a correct determination of *p*'s truth. If my assent to *p* is decisive, there is, from my point of view, no epistemic need for such a discussion. So the appeal to methodological conservatism fails. (Similarly, if an appeal is made to methodological conservatism as justified by our pragmatic argument, the point would be that the prudential or moral goods to be attained by religious belief do not require decisive assent.)

Regarding the second claim, a belief is religious not only in virtue of its content (e.g., the fact that it is about God) but also in virtue of the way it functions in the life of one who holds it. There are at least three reasons for thinking that this function requires decisive rather than interim assent to the belief. First, religious belief represents the (relative) end of a quest for emotional and intellectual satisfaction. There is much that believers still fail to understand and much that they still desire; but they are entirely confident in their belief as a firm basis for the further pursuit of their quest. This viewpoint is strikingly present even in Augustine's famous expression of the restlessness of the believer who does not yet rest (in heaven) with God:

> Thou didst call and cry out and burst in upon my deafness; Thou didst shine forth and glow and drive away my blindness; Thou didst send forth Thy fragrance, and I drew in my breath and now I pant for Thee; I have tasted, and now I hunger and thirst; Thou didst touch me, and I was inflamed with desire for Thy peace.[9]

As a believer, Augustine longs and hopes for God; he is on

the path, not yet arrived. But even so, his longing and un-
rest derive from a decisive encounter with the divine reality
that Augustine expresses in the language of direct sensory
experience. He longs so achingly for God precisely because
he has unequivocally seen, heard, and tasted God's presence. It is absurd to think of Augustine's longing as deriving
from an interim commitment to God's reality maintained
for the sake of someday coming to a decisive conclusion
about the matter. Of course, not every believer will have
had Augustine's quasi-sensory encounter with God. But
any religious belief worthy of the name must surely call
for and legitimate a longing for God as the all-dominating
longing of the believer's life, the believer's "master passion."
By contrast, the life of a believer who gave only interim
assent to God's reality on the grounds of methodological
conservatism could be rightly dominated not by the longing for God but, at best, only by the longing to *know*
whether or not God exists.

Secondly, what is believed religiously requires a total
commitment to its implications for action that is incompatible with continuing reflection on its truth. Thus, at
least as far as the fundamental content of their faith is
concerned, believers should be prepared to forego any
earthly good and to run any temporal risk for the sake of
what they believe. It is true that acting with total commitment to a belief does not require absolute certainty about
the belief. I can rightly give my life for a belief that I
acknowledge as merely probable and that I admit I might
give up on the basis of new evidence. But this does not
show that the commitment is consistent with interim
assent, because we can give decisive assent to a belief that
we find merely probable and subject to future rejection.
Decisive assent is not an assertion of certainty but only of
the lack of a present need to continue the project of inquiry. Further, the very meaning of decisive assent shows
that it is necessary for total commitment. Even though I
can rightly, for example, sacrifice my life or my fortune

for a belief about which I am not entirely certain, it is simply foolish to give up everything for a belief that I think requires further discussion and evaluation. The very fact that I act so decisively on a belief requires that my assent be decisive.

Thirdly, a merely interim assent is inconsistent with the typically religious attitude toward nonbelief. A believer may agree that nonbelievers need not be culpable for their nonbelief; they may, in the traditional phrase, be "invincibly ignorant," lacking faith through no fault of their own and in this sense subjectively justified in their nonbelief. But believers must also assert the superiority of their belief and see even justified nonbelief as an unfortunate fact. For the believer, the world would be a far better place if everyone could see his way to accepting the believer's faith. By contrast, those who give merely interim assent to a belief must recognize the equal value, as an essential element in the continuing discussion, of beliefs contrary to theirs. Their adherence to their belief is combined with an acknowledgment of the need for others to adhere to its denial. Interim assent cannot proclaim the ideal of its belief as "the one thing needful."

I conclude, then, that although there is a viable principle of methodological conservatism, it does not justify religious belief in the ordinary sense of the term. (More precisely, it may justify holding beliefs with a religious content, but it will not justify holding them in a religious way.) If there is nothing more in the way of a justification available for religious beliefs, it will be necessary to rethink their significance in human affairs, taking account of the fact that they deserve no more than interim assent. I suspect that even under these conditions they would be entitled to a major role in human lives and culture. But before retrenching, we need to see if religious beliefs can be decisively justified in any other way. This will be the concern of part II.

PART II
Justifying Religious Beliefs

There is a variety of logically distinct ways in which a case may be made for religious belief. The basic division is between cases that offer evidence for the truth of religious claims and those that do not. Here we may speak of truth-oriented vs. truth-independent cases or justifications; or – to adopt terminology used in discussions of induction – justification vs. vindication. Our concern in part I centered on truth-independent cases, of which we have seen several instances: attempts to exhibit religious beliefs as properly basic, divided into those based on the claim (of the Wittgensteinians) that the question of justification *cannot* be properly raised and those based on the claim (of Plantinga) that the question of justification *need not* be raised; defenses of religious belief, in the sense of the mere refutation of objections; appeal to methodological conservatism, whereby the mere fact of holding a belief is offered as a basis for holding it. Since our conclusion has been that none of the truth-independent approaches is successful, we need now to turn to the more traditional project of providing evidence for the truth of religious claims.

Here we encounter much ground that is all-too-familiar,

and I am as reluctant as the reader to reenter the dusty paths of traditional apologetics. I am also, however, convinced that there are some less noted paths that promise fruitful new perspectives. These are paths that avoid what seems to be the common failing of the more standard attempts to justify religious belief: the assumption that religious claims (particularly theism) can be established by a single, definitive argument — a clearly contained, exhaustively formulable set of premises entailing the proposition that God exists. There is good reason to think that the search for a single master argument of this sort is in vain.

But there are other kinds of arguments, inductive in a broad sense, that support their conclusions not by threat of logical contradition or incoherence but by a marshalling of a large, diverse, and indefinitely extendible body of data, pointing as a whole to its conclusion. As an example, consider the difference between a chemist's argument against attributing a painting to Vermeer on the grounds that standard chemical tests show the pigment to have been manufactured two hundred years after his death, and an art critic's argument against attribution on the grounds of diverse historical, biographical and stylistic considerations. The latter sort of argument has two distinctive features. First, unlike ordinary deductive arguments and many inductive ones, individual premises, taken by themselves, are not necessary for the argument's success; there is a sufficient amount of supportive evidence that the bracketing or rejection of part of it is not decisive. For this reason, this sort of argument may be called multidimensional in contrast to the unidimensionality of arguments that depend on a single chain of premises. Second, accepting the premises of a multidimensional argument does not *compel* us to the conclusion under pain of logical incoherence. Rather, accepting and reflecting on the premises *puts us in a position* to judge that the conclusion is true, without logically forcing the judgment. These two features make multidimensional arguments particularly suited for the justification of religious beliefs. The first provides a stability of conviction that allows believers to continue in their faith even when they come to see the inadequacy of some aspects of its support. The second provides the basis for a distinction between faith (which is generally thought to involve volition) and a coerced, nonvolitional knowledge.

There are two particularly important types of multi-dimensional arguments. The first treats its conclusion as an *explanatory hypothesis* that receives diverse support from its ability to make sense of a wide variety of phenomena. Thus, a comprehensive scientific theory is preferred over a rival, not in virtue of any single crucial experiment but because of a multitude of superiorities in its way of accounting for the facts of their domain. In the second, the conclusion is not a hypothesis but the apparent deliverance of immediate experience, supported first by the experience itself and secondly by a variety of further experiences that we expect to have if the initial experience is veridical. Thus, I seem to see my wife walking up our driveway and this impression is corroborated by subsequent experiences of her appearance close up, her voice, her laugh, and so on. The claim that my wife is home is not a hypothesis inferred from its explanatory power; but there is a wide variety of evidence that justifies my belief in this claim and hence there is a multidimensional justification of it.

Both these forms of multidimensional justification seem to be available for religious belief. The hypothetical-explanatory sort of justification is most prominent in some recent suggestions that a quasi-scientific case can be made for theism. It is, of course, not surprising that our discussions of the justification of religious belief are inevitably and strongly influenced by the science that is our paradigmatic source of rational justification. Both believers and their critics have traditionally invoked the authority of science, its methods as well as its results. In recent years, the sword of science has been mainly wielded by critics of religion; philosophical discussions, in particular, have been dominated by challenges to religious belief based on standards of meaning and justification derived from analyses of scientific methodology. It has, for example, been argued that, if religious beliefs, like scientific ones, express factual claims about the world, then they must in principle be falsifiable by experience. Given this, believers are presented with a dilemma: if their beliefs are falsifiable, then it seems clear that they have been falsified or, at best, that there is insufficient evidence for them. If their beliefs are not falsifiable, then they do not express literal truths about the world but are at best symbolic expressions, perhaps of moral norms or aesthetic ideals. The most common responses to this challenge have grasped the second horn of the dilemma, admitting that the meaning and justification of religious claims are very different from that of scientific claims and arguing that this fact is consistent with (or even necessary for) the true and traditional significance of religious beliefs. However, some recent defenders of religious belief have noted that the standard challenges are based on empiricist views of science that postpositivist philosophy of science has severely criticized. They have further suggested that these criticisms lead to new conceptions of scientific justification that can be successfully applied to a defense of religious belief. In this way, the two-edged nature of the appeal to science is once more apparent, as believers urge that, properly understood, the same methods that justify scientific theories can be used to justify religious belief.

Thomas Kuhn's antipositivist account of science has been the main support of this new approach to the justification of religious belief, the suggestion being that, if we adopt a Kuhnian view of science, then the same kind of processes used to justify scientific claims can be used to justify religious claims. In chapter 4 I examine this suggestion in some detail. I first reflect on the proposals that Basil Mitchell and Ian Barbour have made regarding a Kuhnian justification of religious belief. Although Mitchell and Barbour show some important parallels between religion and Kuhnian science, they fail to take account of the central feature of Kuhn's view of scientific justification: its ultimate foundation in a *consensus* of judgment among scientists. Because religion has been incapable of generating the relevant sort of consensus, Kuhn's concept of a paradigm and the attendant notion of rational authority based on consensus cannot be extended to religious belief. The most that can be salvaged from the parallel with Kuhnian science is the idea (available in any case from other sources) of a justification of religious belief by a cumulative case, rather than a single master argument. But upon examination, the force of such a cumulative case turns out to be very weak.

The approach of Mitchell and Barbour treats religious beliefs as hypotheses to be supported by a cumulative evidential case. Believers often suggest, however, that their most basic beliefs are for them much more like immediate experiential givens than indirectly confirmed hypotheses. Further, the epistemological criticism put forward by Kuhn and many others has neutralized the positivist doctrines about the nature of experience that would make a direct experience of religious realities inconceivable. Accordingly, I turn in chapter 5 to the attempt to base religious belief directly on experience. I try to show that there is, in fact, good reason to think that religious experiences of one rather common sort — awarenesses of the direct presence of God — are veridical. The veridicality of such experiences provides justification for decisive assent to the central religious assertion that there is a good and powerful nonhuman being who cares about us. Given this as a "core" of religious belief, I argue that the far stronger assertions of traditional religions can be added on as an "outer belt," worthy of only interim assent, but playing a crucial role in the believer's assent to the hard core.

4. Paradigms and Religious Beliefs

1. Mitchell and Barbour on the Justification of Religious Belief

According to Basil Mitchell,[1] there are meager prospects for justifying religious belief (or disbelief) by any single decisive deductive or inductive argument. All the traditional apologetic proofs (of God's existence, immortality, the veracity of the Gospels, etc.) can be shown to fail as arguments. However, Mitchell also thinks that it is possible to employ many of the considerations at work in the traditional proofs (along with other considerations) to make a "cumulative case" for religious belief — specifically, Christianity:

> What has been taken to be a series of failures when treated as attempts at purely deductive or inductive argument could well be understood as contributions to a cumulative case. On this view, the theist is urging that traditional Christian theism makes better sense of all the evidence available than does any alternative on offer, and the atheist is contesting the claim [*The Justification of Religious Belief,* pp. 39–40].

Mitchell suggests how such a cumulative case might be developed:

Prima facie the elements of the theistic scheme do tend to rein-
force one another. . . . Thus, although the cosmological and
teleological arguments do not . . . prove that there must be a
transcendent creator of the world, they do make explicit one
way (arguably the best way) in which the existence and nature
of the universe can be explained, if indeed they can be explained
at all. The atheist is entitled . . . to deny that the universe requires
explanation, and so long as the matter is left there, the theist's
far-ranging claims can rest on nothing more than the abstract
consideration that explanation is to be sought wherever possible.
But when there is brought into the reckoning the claim of some
men to be aware of the presence of God, and of others to have
witnessed the action of God in the world or to have been ad-
dressed by him, the case is altered. . . . If there were a God who
had created the universe in which there could develop rational
beings capable of responding to him and to one another with
love and understanding, it is to be anticipated that he would
in some way communicate with them. The existence, then, of
what purport to be such 'revelations' is something which tends
to support the belief in a God who has in these ways revealed
himself [pp. 40–42].

Mitchell's concern, however, is not to develop a cumulative case for Christianity but to show the appropriateness
of employing this method of justification to issues of
religious belief. He begins by showing how the method
does function in other contexts – the interpretation of
poetry and controversies about history – as a rational
means of adjudication. A hypothesis about an author's
intentions in writing a poem, for example, can be established by showing how it makes the best overall sense of
specific passages in the poem, the poem's relation to the
rest of the author's work, relevant incidents in the author's
life, and so forth. However, Mitchell notes, it might seem
that a cumulative case can be effectively developed in such
instances only because all reasonable competing hypotheses
are derived from the same basic conceptualization of the

situation (the poem has an author who is in many relevant ways like other human beings, it is constructed according to certain established literary conventions, etc.). It remains to be shown that the method can be applied in cases, like that of religious belief, where alternative views are based on radically different conceptualizations.

It is at this point that Mitchell appeals to Kuhn's account of science. For, he argues, Kuhnian scientific revolutions are examples of radical conceptual changes that are justified not by ordinary deductive or inductive arguments but by a cumulative case. The radicalness of revolutionary changes is apparent in three features that, Mitchell points out, are also characteristic of debates between theists and atheists. First, there is the fact that, as Kuhn says, scientific "schools guided by different paradigms are always slightly at cross-purposes. . . . They are bound to talk through one another. . . . They will often disagree about the list of problems that any candidate for paradigm must solve."[2] "This," Mitchell says, "reminds one strikingly of the situation in which thesists and atheists do not agree either as to what are the problems to be solved, or as to the characterization of the 'facts' or the 'evidence'" (*The Justification of Religious Belief,* p. 69). Secondly, Mitchell notes that, on Kuhn's view, "when a paradigm shift occurs, a comparatively large-scale transformation of the individual's 'world' takes place" (e.g., when scientists changed from a Newtonian to an Einsteinian worldview); and, he says, "the parallel with religious conversion is too obvious to require elaboration" (p. 70). Thirdly, Mitchell points out that the language Kuhn uses "to describe the experience of undergoing a paradigm shift is strongly reminiscent of the language of religious conversion" ("scales falling from the eyes," "a lightning flash," etc.) and that Kuhn in fact actually describes individuals' moves from one paradigm to another as being like religious conversions.

Mitchell notes, however, that a critic could admit these similarities between religious and scientific "conversions" but reject the rationality of both sorts of changes. After all, one of the most common criticisms of Kuhn is that on his account scientific paradigm changes are irrational; if so, the same will no doubt be true of decisions to accept or reject a religious view. Mitchell responds to this crucial objection by analyzing the two Kuhnian theses that might seem to entail an irrationalist view of science: (1) that there are no paradigm-independent facts; and (2) that different paradigms employ different criteria of evaluation in assessing evidence. Regarding (1), Mitchell says that "the claim . . . that proponents of different scientific paradigms do not agree as to what constitutes 'the facts' is true only up to a point" (p. 79). There is disagreement about the characterization of *some* facts, but the disagreement takes place in the framework of substantial agreement about many scientific and commonsense facts. This is not to deny that all facts are to some extent theory-laden. But, Mitchell claims, even two rival paradigms will see many facts through the lenses of similar theoretical interpretations. These mutually acknowledged facts provide a body of "data" that rival paradigms try to explain; the more of them a given paradigm explains, the stronger the cumulative case for it.

Even with some agreement as to the facts that need explaining, there could be no rational choice between paradigms if proponents of each were in complete disagreement about the criteria for a good explanation. This is why thesis (2) seems to be at odds with the rationality of science. Mitchell, however, points out that Kuhn does not hold that *all* evaluative criteria in science are paradigm-relative. He recognizes a variety of paradigm-independent criteria (e.g., accuracy, scope, simplicity, and fruitfulness) that will be accepted by all parties to any paradigm dispute. But the threat of irrationalism reappears because of Kuhn's insistence that the criteria for evaluating rival paradigms do not provide *rules* dictating the choice that should be made. As Kuhn puts it:

> What I am denying then is neither the existence of good reasons nor that these reasons are of the sort usually described. I am, however, insisting that such reasons constitute values to be used in making choices rather than rules of choice. . . . Simplicity, scope, fruitfulness and even accuracy can be judged quite differently (which is not to say they may be judged arbitrarily) by different people. Again, they may differ in their conclusions without violating any accepted rule.[3]

Kuhn's critics, Mitchell says, assume that only a choice determined by rules can be rational, and so conclude that his account entails irrationalism. Kuhn himself rejects the charge of irrationalism; but, because he insists that paradigm choices can be understood only in psychological or sociological terms, Mitchell thinks he can call them rational only in a Pickwickian sense. However, Mitchell argues that there is room for a notion of rationality that lies between logical derivation and psycho-social determination; and that this notion applies to the process, so well described by Kuhn, by which the cumulative case for a paradigm leads the scientific community to accept it. Accordingly, Mitchell concludes that Kuhn's account of science does present us with a case in which major conceptual changes can be rationally justified by a cumulative case. Given this, there is in principle no obstacle to a cumulative justification of religious belief. If the justification cannot be carried out, this will be because religious claims in fact happen to be the best explanation of the "data" they try to account for.

Ian Barbour's view of the basic epistemology of science and religion is very similar to Mitchell's.[4] He presents a position that he thinks "incorporates . . . the most significant insights of Kuhn's reformulated position and the most important contributions of his critics" (*Myths, Models, and Paradigms,* p. 112). He summarizes his view in three theses. (1) "All data are theory-laden but rival theories are not incommensurable." This is because, although "there is no pure observation language . . . , protagonists of rival theories can seek a common core of overlap in observation languages, on a level closer to agreed observations to which both can retreat" (p. 133). (2) "Comprehensive theories are highly resistant to falsification, but observation does exert some control over them" (p. 114). Such theories are not liable to refutation by a single anomaly, "but an accumulation of anomalies, or of *ad hoc* modifications having no independent experimental or theoretical basis cannot be tolerated indefinitely" (p. 114). (Barbour also emphasizes that the rejection of a theory must always be in favor of a more adequate rival.) (3) "There are no rules for choice between research programmes [or paradigms], but there are independent criteria of assessment" (p. 115). Barbour cites the same sort of criteria referred to by Mitchell (accuracy, scope, simplicity, etc.) and also says that although "there are no rules . . . for the unambiguous application of the criteria . . . the criteria provide what Kuhn calls 'shared values' and 'good reasons' for choice" (p. 115). It is clear that the first and third of these theses correspond almost exactly to Mitchell's interpretation of the two Kuhnian theses discussed above. And the second of Barbour's theses implicitly expresses Mitchell's view that scientific theories can be accepted or rejected on the basis of a cumulative case for or against them. (In fact, in a later explication of this thesis, he explicitly speaks of "the cumulative effect of evidence for or against a theory" [p. 145].)

Barbour also agrees with Mitchell that these three theses are valid for religion as well as for science. He acknowledges that in the case of religion the "subjective features" expressed by each thesis are more pronounced (i.e., there is more influence of theory on data, greater resistance to falsification, less role for rules of choice); but he emphasizes that in all cases the difference is only one of degree, "not an absolute contrast between an 'objective' science and a 'subjective' religion" (p. 145).

Barbour's discussion, however, goes beyond Mitchell's in one very important respect. In Kuhn's own account, his central epistemological theses (about theory-laden observations, resistance of theories to falsification, etc.) are primarily supported by his model of scientific change. The central element of this model is the notion of a *paradigm*, best understood in terms of Kuhn's initial definition: "universally recognized scientific achievements that for a time provide model problems and solutions to a community of practitioners."[5] *Normal science* is the effort to extend the achievement of the paradigm by using its resources to solve new problems; *anomalies* are failures of proposed solutions to problems; a *crisis* occurs when we begin to think that an accumulation of anomalies is due to basic inadequacies in the paradigm; and a crisis is resolved by *revolution* when a new paradigm emerges to replace the old as a basis for normal science. It is because of this central role of the paradigm in the development of science that there are no theory-free observations (all data are given in terms of the paradigm's theoretical categories); that comprehensive theories are resistant to falsification (normal science assumes that failures are due to our lack of skill or persistence, not to the falsity of the paradigm's central theoretical claims); and that theory-choice is not determined by methodological rules (the criteria implicit in a paradigm cannot be entirely explicated by a list of rules).

Barbour completes the analogy to Kuhnian science by showing how the notion of paradigm can be applied to religion. His definition of paradigm is "a tradition transmitted through historical exemplars" (p. 113). This characterization differs from Kuhn's, cited above, in that it identifies a paradigm with the tradition associated with a "universally recognized scientific achievement" (i.e., an exemplar) rather than with this achievement itself. Nevertheless, the two definitions are compatible: what Barbour calls a "tradition" is just the general scientific worldview (basic laws, ontology, methodology, etc.) that is implicit in a specific scientific achievement (e.g., Newton's work in mechanics) and hence accepted by the community that recognizes the achievement as a model for its practice. It is however, essential to recognize that the general worldview (tradition) cannot be completely expressed as an explicitly formulated set of propositions and rules and is most basically given only through the concrete instance of the exemplar.

Working in terms of Barbour's definition, it would seem that a religious worldview can be rightly characterized as a paradigm provided it meets two key conditions: (1) to accept it is to be a member of a specific community; (2) it is accepted through a recognition of certain past achievements as exemplars for the life of the community. Barbour claims that both these conditions are satisfied by religious worldviews:

> Neither religion nor science is an individual affair. Religion is corporate; even the contemplative mystic is influenced by a historical tradition. No one adheres to science or religion in general; the initiate joins a particular community and adopts its modes of thought and action. . . .
>
> The key events remembered by a community help to define its self-identity. Kuhn seems to hold that the exemplars are edited and perhaps idealized versions of historical accomplishments which appear in textbooks, rather than the actual historical events themselves. Events in the lives of Moses, Buddha and Christ play somewhat similar roles in the self-definition of religious communities. . . . Furthermore, religious traditions, unlike scientific ones, are often totally and explicitly organized around the memory of their historical exemplars as individual persons. Particular aspects of their lives serve as norms for the community's life and thought [pp. 133–34].

Barbour further notes that a tradition must not be thought of as "an unchanging legacy from the past" and that "a community can understand its exemplar and its historic origins in new ways and can adapt to new circumstances and new problems" (p. 149). Certainly, the Kuhnian model of science is a developmental one and so will apply only to communities for which tradition has this dynamic nature. Barbour contends that religious traditions are of this sort:

> In modern times all the major religious traditions have gone through changes of unprecedented magnitude. As compared to scientific communities, religious communities are more dominated by the past and more reluctant to accept new ideas, but once again these are differences of degree rather than sharp contrast [p. 149].

2. Difficulties Facing a Kuhnian Justification of Religious Belief

Mitchell and Barbour have exhibited a number of suggestive parallels between religion and Kuhnian science. They pass over, however, one crucial respect in which Kuhn's account cannot be extended to religion; and this ignored disanalogy undermines their central claim that the same essential pattern of justification is at work in both science and religion.

The crucial disanalogy derives from one of Kuhn's most important contributions: his proposal of a new interpretation of the authority of science. On his interpretation, the authority of science resides ultimately not in a rule-governed method of inquiry whereby scientific results are obtained but in the scientific community that obtains the results. It is, of course, always possible to formulate abstractly a variety of "rules"(empirical and theoretical laws, experimental techniques, methodological directives, and even metaphysical principles) that govern the practice of science. But, Kuhn insists, any such rules are relevant to the practice of science only to the extent that they are embodied in some concrete scientific achievement (paradigm) and that this achievement is not reducible to the rules implicit in it.

Many of Kuhn's most important (and controversial) claims about scientific revolutions derive from his attempt to show that the acceptance of a new paradigm is not simply a matter of applying rules. This is particularly true of his thesis that competing paradigms are "incommensurable" with one another. As Mitchell and Barbour note, incommensurability does not mean that rival paradigms cannot be comparatively evaluated. The point of saying that rival paradigms are incommensurable is to point out that scientific judgments of their relative merits are not just a matter of applying rules that could *prove* one paradigm superior to another. As Kuhn says, "Just because it is a transition between incommensurables, the transition between paradigms cannot be made a step at a time, forced by logic and neutral experience."[6] This is not to say that the judgment in favor of a given paradigm is arbitrary and irrational: ". . . to say that . . . paradigm changes cannot be justified by proof, is not to say that no arguments are relevant. . . ."[7] Kuhn thinks, for example, that arguments for the superior problem-solving resources of a paradigm are particularly important. But the incommensurability of rival paradigms means that the ultimate issue of debates about them will depend on the scientific community's judgment as to the overall significance of the considerations urged by the various conflicting arguments. Given that scientists are specifically trained to make fair and informed judgments of this sort, Kuhn asks, "What better criterion than the decision of the scientific group could there be?"[8] This emphasis on the scientific community's judgment as the ultimate locus of the rational authority of science is a central feature of his account of science.[9]

This interpretation of scientific authority is necessarily based on the fact that scientific communities do reach a common judgment about which theories should be used as a basis for exploring a given scientific domain; the mark of a scientific community is consensus about a paradigm. Without such consensus, there would be no unified judgment of the scientific community that could be put forward as authoritative. Because of this, the Kuhnian account of scientific cognitive authority cannot be extended to religion, where there are a wide variety of competing paradigms, without the consensus needed for a cognitively authoritative judgment. There is, of course, consensus within specific groups (individual churches or sects). But taking the judgment of any one such group as authoritative is arbitrary, since there is no reason for preferring its judgment to that of numerous other groups. This situation contrasts sharply with that of scientific communities, whose judgments are shared by almost all those competent in the subject-matter. The contrast is further apparent in the fact that revolutions in religion, unlike science, are hardly ever a matter of one and the same community's abandoning an old paradigm for a new one, but of a community's splitting into two, one accepting a new paradigm, the other maintaining the old. Religious paradigms are essential to the identity of the communities that hold them in a way that scientific paradigms are not. (Fundamental religious beliefs seem to be more like the basic values — predictive accuracy, explanatory fruitfulness, etc. — that Kuhn sees as essential to the scientific enterprise as such.) It might be possible to establish the superiority of the judgment of some particular religious group (e.g., by showing that it has received a special revelation from God); but then the authority of the group will derive from the considerations put forward to establish the superiority of its judgment, not from the fact of a consensus among its members.

Of course, beneath sectarian differences on specific

doctrinal points, we can almost always find agreement at a more general level. This suggests that, even if Kuhn's account of cognitive authority cannot be applied to specific sects, it might apply to more broadly characterized religious communities — Christians rather than Baptists or Catholics, or perhaps even the community of theists or religious believers in general. One obvious difficulty with this move is that there is lack of consensus even on the level of these much larger communities. There is no more reason to prefer the judgment of the community of Christians to that of the community of Hindus than there is to prefer the judgment of Baptists to that of Episcopalians. Even on the very broadest level, why should we believe that the consensus among theists is more authoritative than that among atheists or agnostics?

But there is another, deeper difficulty. Not just any worldview that receives some widespread acceptance is a paradigm. A paradigm must also provide a basis for an ongoing activity of problem-solving in the community that accepts it. Only a succession of successful problem solutions can provide the cumulative evidence that the community needs to form its judgment of the paradigm's continuing acceptability. But this means that a paradigm must be specific enough to generate problems and to suggest determinate solutions to them. Thus, we can speak of the kinetic theory but not the general thesis of atomism as a paradigm in physics. The former raises numerous questions (e.g., How do collisions among the molecules of a gas affect its observable behavior?) and gives us concrete ideas of how to answer them; the latter at best suggests a general direction in which problems and solutions might be sought. Similarly a religious viewpoint that truly functions as a paradigm must generate a significant body of problems and solutions. The views that define specific sects do function in this way; they continually respond to challenges from secular knowledge (e.g., evolution, historical studies of the Bible) and from moral and social issues (e.g., population control, political revolutions). By contrast, there are hardly any problems posed by theism, taken as the widely accepted claim that there is a being of unlimited power and goodness who created and controls the universe. Certainly, such a view has scant revelance to social and moral issues, because it tells us nothing of any moral directives or sanctions laid down by God and nothing of his involvement in the affairs of human beings. Further, a confrontation of theism with secular knowledge yields little in the way of problems and solutions. There is, of course, the problem of the existence of evil in a world governed by an all-powerful and all-good God. But though we can perhaps show the possibility of a world with both God and evil by analyzing the claims of theism (as Plantinga does in his free-will defense), a full-blooded explanation of evil requires a much more specific account of human existence and God's providence than mere theism provides. Even if we augment theism with the claim that God has revealed himself to us in the person of Christ and that this revelation is essentially contained in the New Testament (thus formulating basic Christianity), there is very little advance in problems and their solutions. Significant bodies of problems and solutions derive only from specific claims about the content of Christ's revelations to us; and here there is little or no agreement among the variety of Christian sects. As a generic viewpoint, Christianity adds nothing to theism beyond an acknowledgment of the reality and authority of Christ. It does not include the specifications of the nature of his reality and the content of his teachings that are needed to generate a problem-solving tradition.

The fact that very general viewpoints such as theism and Christianity do not function as paradigms is further apparent in the fact that they alone have never sustained the life of any significant religious communities. Theism and Christianity are social realities only in the sense that they form part of the beliefs of existing communities. In themselves, they are abstractions that do not correspond to any groups of significantly interacting persons. Religion as a social reality exists only in particular churches and sects. Because Kuhn's paradigms require the allegiance of concretely existing communities, his account cannot be extended to religious social abstractions such as theism and Christianity.

For the above reasons, Mitchell's and Barbour's claim that religious belief can be justified in ways essentially similar to those employed in science fails. Kuhn's account of scientific justification is ultimately rooted in the consensus of scientific communities; no parallel consensus exists in religion. It might, however, be suggested that Mitchell and Barbour have at least shown that science employs a method of cumulative argumentation that is also available for religious claims. But surely the rational authority of a cumulative case is peculiarly dependent on its power to generate consensus among competent judges. Even in the cases of history and literary criticism cited by Mitchell, the ultimate acceptability of an interpretation depends on its ability to persuade the great majority of the relevant experts. When a cumulative case generates no consensus, only epistemic egoists will prefer their own judgment; and we saw in chapter 3 the severe limitations of such a position.

But, even apart from such considerations, there remains the question of whether, in our own judgment, a plausible cumulative case for religious belief can be constructed. (Although they defend the project, neither Mitchell nor Barbour in fact develops such a case.) In the following section I argue that the prospects for an effective cumulative case for even so minimal a claim as basic theism are very dim.

3. The Cumulative Case for Theism

Let us see what sort of cumulative case might be made for theism, taken again as the belief that there is an all-powerful and all-good creator and governor of the universe. A cumulative case is based on the ability of a view to explain a certain range of facts. In the case of theism, these facts seem to be of four main sorts. First, there are *cosmological facts* — for example, the existence of the universe, and the order and design manifest in it — that are the basis for the main causal arguments for God's existence. Secondly, there are specifically *religious facts* — experiences of a divine power, apparently miraculous events, the very fact that religions exist and command the allegiance of so many — that seem to reveal specific interventions of God in human history. Thirdly, there are *moral facts*, the experiences of obligation, guilt, and reconciliation that sustain our commitment to a moral order. Finally, there are *personal facts* — for example, meeting a particular person at a crucial time, an unexpected job offer, an illness that transforms one's outlook on life — that can be interpreted as God's providential intervention into the lives of individuals.

The claim is that theism explains all these facts. But before we evaluate this claim, we need to note some importantly different ways in which an account (A) can be said to explain a fact (F). A explains F in a *strong sense* if, given A and further assumptions that we have good reason to think are true, it is reasonable to think that F obtains. A explains F in a *weak sense* if, given A, it is reasonable to think that F obtains only if we add further assumptions that may well be true but that we have no good reason to think are true (i.e., there is, overall, no adequate basis for thinking the assumptions are true but no adequate basis for thinking they are false). Ordinarily, a cumulative case for A requires showing that it strongly explains at least some facts in its domain. However, a good case can be made for an A that only weakly explains, provided it can be shown that it is the *only* explanation (even in the weak sense) of some of the facts it explains; or, at least, that it is the best of the available weak explanations.

One major obstacle facing a cumulative case for theism is that it does not strongly explain any of the facts in its domain. Consider, for example, the cosmological fact of the world's existence. We know that an omnipotent being could create the world if it so willed; and so, given the existence of God and the fact that he wills to create the world, the world's existence follows directly. But what could be our basis for assuming that an all-good and all-powerful being would choose to create this world? It has been suggested that an all-good being would want to share its goodness by creating other beings; but, on the other hand, it could as well be argued that an all-good being would not create any world, since any creature will be finite and imperfect. But in any case we have no reason for thinking that God would have chosen to create *this* world.

More generally, theistic explanations of any of the classes of facts listed above require assumptions about what God would want or how he would act. Thus, an explanation of religious experiences assumes he would want to communicate with us, an explanation of moral experience that he would try to help us be good, etc. But it is hard to see how we could have reason to think that God will have any specific intentions or will act in any specific way. We can, of course, say that he will always intend the best goal and act for this in a maximally effective way. But precisely because we lack his omniscience, we have no way of judging what specifically he would be likely to do. Any such judgments must be ultimately based on what we (or a moral idealization of ourselves) would do (if we could), given our understanding of the situation. But our understanding of anything will at best be only a dim reflection of God's, and so there is no reason to think that our judgment would coincide with his. We know how far wrong we would go by inferring the likely behavior of a wise adult from the judgments of even the best-intentioned child as to what ought to be done; and the distance between God and man is immeasurably greater than that between a child and even the wisest adult.

Furthermore, it seems that theists themselves must appeal to the inscrutability of the divine purpose in order to explain the existence of evil. One of the most effective ways of formulating the problem of evil is to point out that there are situations that, as far as we can tell, could not be permitted by any morally good being that had the power to prevent them (e.g., cases of a small child's dying of cancer in which I would, if I had the power, be obligated to provide a cure). The only way the theist can explain the existence of such situations is by assuming that God in his omniscience has relevant knowledge about the situation that we lack, so that our judgment of what God should do is wrong because it is insufficiently informed.[10] And, if a critic objects that this is an implausible assumption, how can the theist reply except by saying that we never have good reason to think that the standpoint of omniscience would not significantly alter judgments of what should be done? But then the theist must admit that the same principle applies in other cases and hence that our understanding never gives us a basis for anticipating God's actions. As Borges has written, ". . . the machinery of the world is overly complex for the simplicity of men."[11]

It seems, then, that our inability to form plausible assumptions about the specific actions of an omniscient being makes it impossible for theism to explain anything in the strong sense. Could theism nonetheless be shown to be the only explanation (weak or strong) of some crucial facts (e.g., the world's existence, moral experience) that need explanation? This is entirely possible, but then there would be no need for a *cumulative* case for theism. It would be proved by one of the traditional theistic arguments. Assuming, as we are here, that theism requires a cumulative case, the only way such a case can be made is by arguing that theism is the best (weak) explanation of the range of facts in its domain. This is the least powerful way of arguing for an account from its explanatory power; but, if the range of data to be explained is wide and varied, it may yield a convincing case.

At this point, it becomes necessary to compare theism with nontheistic alternatives. These can take various forms, but I shall focus on the most popular generic alternative, naturalism. By naturalism I mean, roughly, the view that the world as a whole is not the result of any purposeful action and that the only purposeful agents that have any important effect on human affairs are human beings themselves. The question we need to ask is, Does naturalism provide at least as good an account as theism of the cosmological, religious, moral, and personal facts on which the cumulative case for theism is based? In order to answer this question, I shall compare theism and naturalism on the basis of four generally accepted fundamental criteria of explanatory adequacy: scope, accuracy, fruitfulness, and simplicity.[12]

With regard to the criterion of scope, the question is, How wide a range of relevant facts can theism and naturalism explain? In the case of two of the classes of facts with which we are concerned (religious and moral experiences), both theism and naturalism seem to have unlimited scope. For both these classes of facts consist of *experiences,* and any experience can, in principle, be produced by either an adequate external cause or appropriate internal psychological factors. Because God is omnipotent, he is always available to explain the occurrence of any experience at all, so the theist will be able to offer an explanation of any moral or religious experience. But the naturalist can likewise explain any experience by invoking one or another of the wide variety of possible psychological causes.

Of course, the mere possibility in principle of an explanation of a given sort does not guarantee the existence of a plausible or probable explanation of the sort required; the scope of an account depends not only on what it can explain but also on what it can plausibly explain (i.e., what it can explain with the aid of further plausible assumptions). However, as we saw above, any theistic explanation depends on assumptions (about God's will) whose plausibility we cannot estimate. So there are no experiences for which theism, considered in itself (i.e., apart from comparisons with other accounts), is a plausible explanation. On the other hand, a theistic explanation is never in itself implausible; so if, in a given case, we can show that naturalistic explanation is implausible, we can judge that theism is the comparatively more plausible explanation. But it is hard to see how we would ever be warranted to conclude that all available psychological and sociological explanations of a religious or moral experience are implausible. The psycho-social mechanisms capable of explaining religious and moral experiences (unconscious desires, wish fulfillment, peer pressure, etc.) are universally available though never directly observable, and it is hard to see how we could have good reason for thinking that they are not operative in a given case unless we had independent reason to think that the experiences had nonnatural causes. So it seems that a naturalistic explanation of a religious or moral experience is never implausible. Accordingly, there is no basis for saying that, with respect to these two sorts of experiences, theism has greater explanatory scope than naturalism.

Regarding the fourth class of facts distinguished above – "personal facts" explainable by divine providence – it is obvious that these are always also explainable by natural causes. And, in fact, it is generally agreed that, without a prior commitment to theism, there is no reason to prefer the providential explanation.

The greater scope of theistic explanation may seem apparent in the case of cosmological facts (the first of the classes distinguished above), because naturalism must, for example, take the existence of the universe as a whole as a brute fact, whereas the theist explains it by God's creative act. However, as debates about cosmological arguments show, the key question is whether the cosmological facts that the theist purports to explain in fact need explanation. It often seems that the explanatory criteria on which cosmological arguments are based are themselves principles peculiar to the conceptual framework of certain types of theism and need not be accepted by those who are not theists. If so, these criteria will be irrelevant to a cumulative case for theism over naturalism. What we need to do, accordingly, is to examine cosmological explanatory criteria to see if they are features not only of theistic conceptual frameworks but also of conceptual frameworks employed by the naturalist.

Cosmological explanatory criteria seem to take one of the following two forms: (1) there is a need for an explanation of the universe (all contingent things taken as a whole), quite apart from particular explanations of the individual things that make up the universe; (2) the complete explanation of any particular thing cannot stop with things that themselves require explanation, but must go on to something that needs no explanation. These principles are often defended as either commonsense truths, implicit in the conceptual framework of ordinary language, or as essential postulates of a scientific approach to the universe. Because naturalism must accept either the conceptual framework of ordinary language or that of science (if not both), a successful defense of the cosmological explanatory principles along these lines will force the naturalist to accept the superior explanatory scope of theism.

With regard to (2): far from being an explanatory principle of either science or ordinary language, this claim is contrary to the explanatory principles of both. A complete explanation (scientific or ordinary) of the existence of a sunflower in my backyard may well require references to the seed from which it grew; but to require reference to the evolutionary emergence of sunflowers in North America would be absurd. As many critics have pointed out, those who think (2) is required are confusing it with the (correct) principle that, given a complete explanation (E) of something, it is generally appropriate to ask for a *further* explanation of the things or facts cited in E.

There is, moreover, a general consideration that I believe shows that neither (1) nor (2) is included in the two conceptual frameworks under consideration. This is the fact that in both frameworks explanatory demands take the form of methodological injunctions rather than ontological presuppositions. That is, we are enjoined to *look* for causes in a wide variety of circumstances, but there is no framework principle to the effect that the sought-after causes will always exist or that they should always be posited. Within the ordinary-language framework, this point is illustrated by our frequent willingness to classify puzzling events or behavior as simply without explanation. (For example, "Why did the soufflé collapse?" "There was no reason — no long wait, sudden jolt, or cold draft; it just happened." Or: "Why doesn't he like ice cream?" "no reason; he just doesn't.") But, it may be objected, is not the scientific framework developed precisely to explain the facts that the ordinary-language framework accepts as ultimate unexplainables? The chef may think there is no explanation for his soufflé's collapse, but the chemist could surely find one; Jones may think there is no reason why he does not like ice cream, but his analyst knows better.

It is true, of course, that the scientist is generally not so readily disposed as the ordinary person to accept facts or events as without explanation; but the scientist is by no means committed in advance to the existence of explanations for everything. This is apparent from the following considerations: In any particular scientific theory, there will be certain facts or events that are unexplained explainers (e.g., in Newtonian mechanics, nonaccelerated motion; in quantum mechanics, an atom's emission of a particular electron; in Freudian psychoanalysis, the id's drives for satisfaction). Scientific methodology is, of course, open to a more fundamental theory that will explain these explanatory ultimates. Thus, after general acceptance of atomic theory, scientists were interested in attempts to account for the properties of atoms (e.g., their stability) on the basis of further postulated entities such as electrons and protons. But the key point for us is that scientists were not prepared to say that a theory postulating such entities was *a fortiori* explanatorily superior to atomic theory by itself. The superiority of elementary-particle theory had to be established by showing that it provided a better account of specific phenomena in the atomic domain. It is the emergence of such accounts and not appeals to general principles about the need for explanations that is the basis of a scientific acceptance of a theory that offers a new level of explanation. Similarly, the fact that theism provides a new level of explanation does not in itself show its explanatory superiority. This superiority can be established only by showing the superiority of theism as an explanation of specific facts in the world.

It seems, then, that neither theism nor naturalism can be judged superior in the scope of the explanations it offers. What about the criterion of accuracy? This criterion is relevant to the evaluation of explanations because no explanation ever gives a complete and entirely precise account of every aspect of its explanandum. There are always features ignored or taken account of only approximately. Consequently, in comparing two explanations of a phenomenon that are successful overall, we often choose between them on the basis of the accuracy with which they account for the details of what they explain. This criterion is particularly important in the natural sciences, where two theories that are both qualitatively correct are judged by the extent of their quantitative accuracy.

In deciding between theism and naturalism, however, appeals to accuracy are of much less importance, since neither viewpoint can be developed with the precision and specificity characteristic of quantified scientific theories. However, to the extent that the criterion of accuracy is relevant, it seems to favor naturalism. Why did Brother Thomas and not Brother John have a vision? Why was the vision of St. Joseph and not of the Blessed Virgin? Why did the vision occur last night and not the night before? Theism alone can never say more than that things happened as they did because that was how God chose to act. Psychological or sociological explanations will typically be able to point to specific factors in an individual's personality or social background that make it more likely that he or she would have a given sort of experience at a given time. Theism can appropriate this explanatory accuracy only by the *ad hoc* assumption that God is more likely to act through or in accord with our psycho-social natures. A genuine increase in theism's explanatory accuracy will often result from adding to basic theism the specific content of some purported revelation of God to us. Typically, such revelations will say that those who follow the creed and practices of a particular religion will be given special aid by and access to God. But even augmented in this way, the explanatory accuracy of theism will be increased only for the cases of those who follow the privileged creed and practices, whereas naturalistic explanations will apply across all religious groups.

The criterion of fruitfulness is also of particular importance in the evaluation of scientific theories. As Kuhn formulates it, this criterion favors theories that "disclose new phenomena or previously unnoted relations among those already known."[13] But fruitfulness, even more than accuracy, seems irrelevant to the choice between theism and naturalism. An account can be fruitful only to the extent that it is *predictive*: only by making predictions can it make us aware of new phenomena or new interrelations of phenomena. But both theism and naturalism are essentially interpretive rather than predictive accounts. They purport to make sense of facts well known in human experience, not to lead us to the experience of new facts.

Finally, there is the amorphous but often very important

consideration of simplicity. As in the case of accuracy, it seems that, to the extent this crierion applies to our case, it favor naturalism over theism. The theist, after all, must agree that the sorts of natural causes to which the naturalist appeals are operative in the world and do provide the correct explanations of many moral, religious, and apparently providential experiences. At the most, the theist holds that some remainder of such experiences needs a nonnatural explanation. So, since the theist admits all the sorts of causes the naturalist does and adds yet another, the theistic account is less simple in one clear sense. There are, of course, particular cases in which the postulation of a further cause effects a net gain in simplicity because without it there is need for a large and complexly related set of explanatory factors. It is, for example, simpler to explain the existence of the carved stones on Easter Island by postulating human artisans than by assuming that they were produced by a spectacular combination of rain, wind, and earthquakes. But naturalistic explanations of religious experiences, etc., do not seem to require an implausibly complex concatenation of natural causes; and, in any case, a theistic explanation of the specifics of such an experience will usually have to rely on the same range of natural causes the naturalist uses to explain the experience as a whole.

I conclude then that, even though there is in principle no obstacle to a cumulative case for theism, the case cannot in fact be made, because theism is not superior in scope, accuracy, fruitfulness, or simplicity to the naturalistic alternative. This conclusion is supported by Richard Swinburne's recent development of a detailed cumulative case for theism. Swinburne tries to show how the probability of the hypothesis of God's existence is increased by the fact that the hypothesis can explain numerous phenomena, such as the existence and design of the world, human and animal consciousness, and the role human beings have in determining their happiness. There are

difficulties with crucial details of specific aspects of
Swinburne's arguments, but even in his own terms it seems
clear that Swinburne's cumulative case by itself fails to justify the claim that God exists. He himself admits this in a
summary passage:

> Theism does not have a probability close either to 1 or 0, that is,
> on the evidence considered so far, theism is neither very probable
> nor very improbable. It does not have a probability close to 1
> because it does not have high predictive power. . . . It is com-
> patible with too much. There are too many different possible
> worlds which a God might bring about. . . . On the other hand,
> theism is a very simple hypothesis with a remarkable ability to
> make sense of what otherwise is extremely puzzling. . . . For this
> reason its probability is not too close to 0.[14]

We are surely not warranted in asserting a proposition so
weakly supported by the relevant evidence.

Interestingly, however, Swinburne sees his cumulative
case as taking on renewed strength when combined with a
case based on experiences of God. He says:

> I concluded the last chapter . . . with the claim that unless the
> probability of theism on other evidence is very low indeed, the
> testimony of many witnesses to experience apparently of God
> suffices to make many of those experiences probably veridical.
> That is, the evidence of religious experience is in that case suf-
> ficient to make theism overall probable. The argument . . . was
> that the testimony of many witnesses to experiences apparently
> of God makes the existence of God probable if it is not already
> on other evidence very improbable. I believe that I have shown in
> this chapter that that condition is well satisfied and hence . . . on
> our total evidence theism is more probable than not.[15]

A cumulative case for theism, with religious experience
just one, dispensable element among many, is not cogent.
But, Swinburne argues, the explanatory cumulative case
(bracketing religious experience) provides an essential
background premise (that theism is not improbable) for an

argument based on religious experience. The possibility that Swinburne is right about this gives us a further reason for moving to the topic of our next chapter.

Before taking up the topic of religious experience, however, I want to say a bit more about the prospects of an explanatory cumulative case for theism. The sort of cumulative case that I have judged a failure is not the only sort possible. It presents theism as competing with naturalistic modes of explanation to account for certain facts about the world. But it may also be possible to allow naturalistic explanations their full scope as complete accounts of the world and what goes on in it, and to introduce theism as a higher level hypothesis designed to answer explanatory questions about the naturalistic explanatory schemata themselves. Here theism would not be treated as a competitor of naturalism but as a complement, supported not by its ability to explain facts about the world that naturalism cannot explain but by its ability to raise and fruitfully answer explanatory questions about the frameworks employed by naturalistic modes of explanation. This would be the sort of method of justification we encountered in chapter 2 as an interpretation of Aquinas's five ways. Aquinas's arguments were not taken as trying to show that, by postulating God, we could explain the ordinary phenomena of the natural world better than we could by applying the standard Aristotelian, Platonic, etc. modes of scientific and philosophical explanation. Rather, they were taken as ways of showing that God could be fruitfully introduced as an explanation of the fundamental categories of these very modes of explanation. Similarly, it might be thought that theism might be introduced today as an explanation of the fundamental categories and ontologies of our current physical, biological, social, and historical modes of explanation.

However, such a project today faces more obstacles than it did in the Middle Ages. For one thing, there is much more variety in the modes of naturalistic explanation, from the mathematical formalisms of physics to the hermeneutics of psychoanalysis. For another, there is much more disagreement regarding the appropriate starting point and available resources for constructing high-level philosophical syntheses. (Indeed, there is significant challenge to the very idea of such projects.) Nonetheless, the twentieth century has produced a few such syntheses that are sufficiently impressive to suggest that the enterprise is not obviously futile. There is, for example, Whitehead's elaboration of a theistic metaphysical scheme that purports to provide the fundamental categories and ontology for making ultimate sense of both our everyday experience and the worldview arrived at by modern physics and biology. There is also Tillich's attempt to present a version of Christianity as the best answer to the deepest existential questions that he finds arising out of all human lives and enterprises. Both these efforts have their problems, both internal and in relation to traditional religoius belief, and their final evaluation would require another book or two. But the continuing intellectual vitality of these and similar efforts at least serves the purpose that Swinburne sees his own version of a cumulative case as serving: they maintain theism as a real possibility in our intellectual world, showing that it is not something we can rule out from the start as utterly implausible. This, as we have noted, is the essential contribution of such arguments to the case — to which we now turn — based on religious experience.

5. The Presence of God and the Justification of Religious Belief

1. Experiences of God

At least since William James' classic work, it has been a commonplace that there are many varieties of religious experience. Oddly, however, philosophical analysts of religious experiences have often ignored this diversity and treated exceptional instances — mystical experiences and physical visions — as typical or even exhaustive of the type. By contrast, I propose to center my discussion on a particular type of religious experience that, though paid little explicit attention by philosophers, is one of the most common and most important in the lives of believers. This is the sort of experience that psychologists of religion call "direct awareness of the presence of God." James gives the following general characterization of such experiences:[1]

> We may lay it down as certain that in the distinctively religious sphere of experience, many persons (how many we cannot tell) possess the objects of their belief, not in the form of mere conceptions which their intellect accepts as true, but rather in the form of quasi-sensible realities directly apprehended [*The Varieties of Religious Experience*, p. 65].

James cites a number of instances of this sort of experience:

> There was not a mere consciousness of something there, but fused in the central happiness of it, a startling awareness of some ineffable good. Not vague either, not like the emotional effect of some poem, or scene, or blossom, or music, but the sure knowledge of the close presence of a sort of mighty person, and after it went, the memory persisted as the one perception of reality. Everything else might be a dream, but not that [p. 63].

> I remember the night, and almost the very spot on the hilltop, where my soul opened out, as it were, into the Infinite, and there was a rushing together of the two worlds, the inner and the outer. . . . I stood alone with Him who had made me, and all the beauty of the world, and love, and sorrow, and even temptation. I did not seek Him, but felt the perfect unison of my spirit with His. . . . The darkness held a presence that was all the more felt because it was not seen. I could not any more have doubted that *He* was there than that I was. I felt myself to be, if possible, the less real of the two [p. 67].

Of the following statement, James says, "Probably thousands of unpretending Christians would write an almost identical account":

> God is more real to me than any thought or thing or person. I feel his presence positively, and the more as I live in closer harmony with his laws as written in my body and mind. I feel him in the sunshine or rain. . . . I talk to him as to a companion in prayer and praise, and our communion is delightful. He answers me again and again, often in words so clearly spoken that it seems my outer ear must have carried the tone, but generally in strong mental impressions [p. 70].

Finally, a few brief statements taken, James says, at random:

> God surrounds me like the physical atmosphere. He is closer to

me than my own breath. In him literally I live and move and have my being.

There are times when I seem to stand in his very presence, to talk with him. Answers to prayers have come, sometimes direct and overwhelming in their revelation of his presence and powers. . . .

I have the sense of a presence, strong, and at the same time soothing, which hovers over me. Sometimes it seems to enwrap me with sustaining arms [p. 71].

More systematic studies reveal the same phenomenon. A recent example is a survey of a random sample of a hundred British university students, two-thirds of whom said they have had religious experiences of some sort, with about one-fourth describing their experiences as "awareness of the presence of God."[2] The following are some representative comments by students reporting such experiences:

It was just about dark and I was looking out of the library window. . . . I was aware of everything going on around me, and I felt that everybody had rejected me — and I felt very alone. But at the same time I was aware of something that was giving me strength and keeping me going . . . protecting me ["Religious Experience Amongst a Group of Post-Graduate Students," p. 168].

It's something that is there all the time. One's awareness of it is limited by one's willingness to submit to it [p. 168].

When I pray . . . I am not praying in a vacuum; there is a response and I feel that at the time of praying, otherwise I think I'd eventually give it up [p. 170].

At university I began to feel the 'gay' life had nothing to offer, life seemed meaningless and all came to a climax about a month before 1st year exams. I was feeling pretty anxious. One night in my room, as I was going to bed, things were at a bursting point. I said, 'I give you my life, whoever you are.' I definitely felt somebody was there and something had been done. I felt relief but not much else, emotionally. It was like a re-direction and this was a gradual thing [pp. 172–73].

There is every reason to believe that at least a very large number of such reports are candid, that the experiences reported did in fact take place. The crucial question is whether any of the experiences are veridical, whether there is reason to think that there really is a powerful and benevolent nonhuman being experienced by people reporting religious experiences. But before discussing this issue, we need to become as clear as possible about the nature of the experiences in question. This is especially important because, as noted above, many philosophical critics of religious experience have simply ignored the existence of the sorts of experiences I have cited. Alasdair MacIntyre, for example, begins his discussion of religious experience by reducing all such experiences ("visions" in his terminology) to two classes:

> . . . first, those visions which can properly be called such, that is, those where something is *seen*; and second, those where the experience is of a feeling-state or of a mental image, which are only called visions by an honorific extension of the term.[3]

He then goes on to argue that religious experiences of the second type could never provide evidence for religious claims because "an experience of a distinctively 'mental' kind, a feeling-state or an image cannot of itself yield us any information about anything other than experience" ("Visions," p. 256). With regard to visions properly speaking, MacIntyre argues that they of course cannot be themselves literally of God, since he cannot be seen, and that we are never warranted in inferring from an X that we see to a Y that we do not see unless we have on other occasions experienced a correlation between X and Y. Whatever we may think of MacIntyre's arguments here (and the second seems particularly weak), it is clear that they do not apply to religious experiences of the sort we are concerned with, since these are neither reports of mere feeling-states or mental images nor claims to have literally seen saints, angels, or the like. Rather, they are experiences that are both *perceptual* (i.e., purporting to be of something other than the experiencer) and *nonsensory* (not of some object of the special senses). As such, they fall into neither of MacIntyre's two classes and so escape the objections he raises.

Similarly, Wallace Matson[4] raises difficulties first for the veridicality of experiences of "voices and visions" and second for "mystical" experiences (i.e., extraordinary encounters that cannot be intelligibly described to those who have not had them). We have already noted that the experiences with which we are concerned are not of "visions or voices." But neither are they the mystic's ineffable raptures. Although they sometimes have aspects their subjects feel cannot be fully described, they can all be adequately if not completely expressed by saying that they are of a very powerful and very good nonhuman person who is concerned about us. Accordingly, Matson's objections to the veridicality of mystical experiences — which all derive from their apparently peculiar ineffability — are irrelevant to the experiences we are concerned with. These, to summarize, are not given as mere feelings or images, nor are they literal physical visions or ineffable mystical insights. Rather, they are perceptual but nonsensory experiences, purporting to be of a good and powerful being concerned with us.

But are these experiences actually of such a being? A first crucial point is that no experience that purports to be of an external object, taken simply by itself, makes it reasonable to believe that there is such an object. There are no "phenomenological" features of an experience that will mark it off as of something real. (This is the valid core of Descartes' dream argument: there may be no intrinsic differences between a veridical and a nonveridical perceptual experience.) Given an experience that purports to be of X, we need to know more before we are entitled to believe that X exists. A useful way of putting this point is as follows: given an experience with X as its *intentional object,* we may still ask if it is reasonable to believe that X exists (that X is a real object). However, for this language not to be misleading, we need to note that saying "E has X as its intentional object" does not mean that X exists in some special nonreal way; rather it means that E has the internal character of being an "of-X" experience; i.e., it is the sort of experience that, if veridical, is of a really existing X.

Given that a religious experience does not wear its veridicality on its sleeve, the central question is how we can move from the experience to its veridicality. Among critics of religious experience, the most common view is that the mere subjective occurrence of an of-God experience is in itself no evidence for God's existence; the fact that the experience has occurred must be supplemented by further premises to form an argument (deductive or inductive) that entails "God exists." Thus, Anthony Flew after noting that "the mere fact of the occurrence of subjective religious experience does not by itself warrant the conclusion that there are any objective religious truths," goes on to say:

> . . . those who propose to rest a lot of weight upon the evidence of religious experience [should] take it as their first and inescapable task to answer the basic question: How and when would we be justified in making inferences from the facts of the occurrence of religious experience, considered as a purely psychological phenomenon, to conclusions about the supposed objective religious truths. . . .[5]

Here Flew misrepresents the epistemic connection between an "of-X" experience and the claim that X exists. This can be most readily seen from the following parody of his statement about religious experience and religious belief:

... those who propose to rest a lot of weight upon the evidence of experiences of material objects should take it as their first and inescapable task to answer the basic question: How and when would we be justified in making inferences from the facts of the occurrence of experiences of material objects, considered as a purely psychological phenomenon, to conclusions about the supposed objective truths about material objects. ...

We have been no more successful at inferring truths about material objects from the subjective occurrence of sense experiences than we have been at inferring truths about God from the subjective occurrence of religious experiences. But no doubts should arise about our belief that sense experiences yield knowledge of material objects, because such experiences do not support these knowledge claims by providing a premise for some master argument against skepticism regarding the senses. Similarly, the failure of religious experiences to ground such an argument does not count against their veridicality. Flew has based his objection on a faulty analysis of the way experiences support objective truth claims.

How, then, do of-X experiences support the claim that X exists? Richard Swinburne[6] has recently suggested that such an experience provides *prima facie* evidence for the claim, evidence that will be decisive if there is not some overriding reason in our background knowledge for questioning the experience's veridicality. He formulates this suggestion in a "Principle of Credulity": "I suggest that it is a principle of rationality that (in the absence of special considerations) if it seems (epistemically) to a subject that X is present, then probably X is present; what one seems to perceive is probably so" (*The Existence of God,* p. 245). The "special considerations" that can impugn the veridicality of an of-X experience are of four sorts. There can be considerations that show: (1) "that the apparent perception was made under conditions or by a subject found in the past to be unreliable" (p. 260); (2) "that the perceptual claim was to have perceived an object of a certain kind in circumstances where similar perceptual claims have proved false" (p. 261); (3) "that on background evidence it is probable that X was not present" (p. 261); (4) "that whether or not X was there, X was probably not a cause of the experience of its seeming to me that X was there" (pp. 263–64). Swinburne argues that none of these conditions are conditions under which we have religious experiences (or receive reports of such experiences); so he concludes that the Principle of Credulity warrants the conclusion that God exists.

Swinburne is right in thinking that to understand properly the epistemic relation between of-X experiences and claims that X exists we need to recognize that the experience is *prima facie* evidence for the claim. But I think he misconstrues the sense in which the experience is *prima facie* evidence. He takes *"prima facie"* to mean that the evidence of the experience is by itself decisive unless there is some overriding consideration in our background knowledge. But this claim is too strong.

Suppose, for example, I walk into my study one afternoon and seem to see, clearly and distinctly, my recently deceased aunt sitting in my chair. We may assume that the conditions of this experience (my mental state, the lighting of the room, etc.) are not ones that we have reason to think produce unreliable perceptions. Thus, the first of Swinburne's defeating conditions does not hold. Nor, given normal circumstances, does the second condition hold. Most likely, I have no knowledge at all of circumstances in which experiences of the dead by apparently normal persons have turned out to be nonveridical. (We may even assume that I have never heard of anyone I regard as at all reliable reporting such an experience.) Further, knowing nothing at all about the habits or powers of the dead, I have no reason to think that my aunt could not now be in my study or, if present, could not be seen by me. So

Swinburne's third and fourth conditions do not hold for this case. But, although none of the four defeating conditions Swinburne recognizes apply, it is obvious that I am not entitled, without further information, to believe that I have in fact seen my aunt. To be entitled to the belief I would need much more evidence — for example, numerous repetitions of the experience, other people having the same or similar experiences, a long visit in which the appearance behaved in ways characteristic of my aunt, information from the appearance that only my aunt had access to, etc. The mere experience described above provides some slight support for the claim that my aunt is in my room, but, even in the absence of defeating conditions, not nearly enough to warrant believing it.

As this example suggests, an of-X experience in general provides *prima facie* evidence of X's existence only in the sense of supplying some (but not sufficient) support for the claim that X exists. For belief in the claim to be warranted, the solitary of-X experience requires supplementation by additional corroborating experiences. It, along with the additional corroboration, provides an adequate cumulative case for the claim. In cases of kinds of objects of which we have frequently had veridical experiences, we can of course rightly believe that they exist, without further corroboration beyond our seeming to see them. But this is because we have good inductive reason to expect that the further corroborations will be forthcoming. With relatively unfamiliar objects — from elves to deceased aunts to divine beings — this sort of inductive reason is not available; and warranted assent must await further corroboration.[7]

Thus, neither Flew's suggestion that an of-X experience by itself has no evidential force, nor Swinburne's that it has sufficient force in the absence of defeating conditions, is adequate. Rather, we should think of an individual of-God experience as providing significant but not sufficient evidence for God's existence, needing to be included in a cumulative body of diverse evidence that can warrant the claim that God exists.

C. B. Martin endorses the sort of view of experiential evidence I am suggesting.[8] He does not require a one-dimensional inference from a subjective experience to its veridicality, but he does insist on the relevance of further "checking procedures" if a subjective experience is claimed to yield an objective truth. For the case of ordinary sense perception (e.g., of a sheet of blue paper), we can, he says, make two sorts of claims. The first is just that the experience as a subjective episode is occurring: "There seems to be a sheet of blue paper." Here the experience is "self-authenticating"; that is, the mere fact of its occurrence is sufficient to establish the truth of the claim based on it. The second sort of claim is that the experience correctly represents an objective state of affairs: "There is a sheet of blue paper." Here, Martin notes, more than just the occurrence of the experience is relevant to the truth of the claim:

> The presence of a piece of blue paper is not to be read off from my experience of a piece of blue paper. Other things are relevant: What would a photograph reveal? Can I touch it? What do others see? It is only when I admit the relevance of such checking procedures that I can lay claim to apprehending the paper, and, indeed, the admission of the relevance of such procedures is what gives meaning to the assertion that I am apprehending the paper. [p. 77].

Presumably, Martin does not mean that, when I have the experience of seeing a piece of paper, I am never entitled to believe that there actually is a piece of paper unless I have in fact carried out further checking procedures. As we have seen, the inductive background of ordinary experience usually obviates the need for such checking. But to claim that the paper is objectively present is to admit the relevance in principle of such checking procedures in the following sense: if such checking procedures should happen not to support the claim, then it becomes questionable; and, if for some reason, the claim is questioned, the procedure can and should be invoked to support it.

It seems to me that Martin, unlike Flew and Swinburne, is employing an essentially correct account of the role of experience in the establishment of objective-truth claims. The main elements of this account are: (1) an "of-X" experience is veridical only if, supposing it to be veridical, we should expect, in suitable circumstances, the occurrence of certain further experiences; (2) if these further experiences do not occur (given the suitable circumstances), we have no basis for accepting the experience as veridical; (3) if, in the relevant circumstances, the experiences occur, we do have a basis for accepting the experience as veridical; (4) if there is some reason for questioning the veridicality of the experience, then appeal to further expected experiences is needed before accepting the experience as veridical.

Since religious beliefs in general and the veridicality of religious experiences in particular are not rationally unquestionable, religious experiences need further corroboration. So here we must, contrary to Swinburne, insist on the need to support the veridicality claim by further checking procedures. Such checking procedures are not further premises in a one-dimensional proof of God's existence; rather, they contribute to a many-dimensional, cumulative experiential case for his reality.

Given this, Martin goes on to claim that in the case of religious experiences of God no further checking procedures are available: "There are no tests agreed upon to establish genuine experience of God and distinguish it decisively from the ungenuine" ("A Religious Way of Knowing," p. 79). Because this is so, he concludes, religious experiences cannot be rightly taken as establishing the objective reality of God; they show nothing besides the existence of certain human psychological states.

What is puzzling here is Martin's assumption that the need for further checking immediately excludes accepting the veridicality of religious experiences. For surely, at least for the class of experiences we are discussing, there are further experiences that would be expected, given their veridicality. Given the veridicality of the typical experience of a very good and very powerful being concerned about us, we would, for example, expect that: (1) those who have had such experiences once would be likely to have them again; (2) other individuals will be found to have had similar experiences; (3) those having such experiences will find themselves aided in their endeavors to lead morally better lives. All these expectations follow from the nature of the experienced being and its concern for us. If the being has soothed, inspired, or warned me once, it is reasonable to expect that it will do so again in appropriate circumstances. If it is concerned enough to contact *me,* it is reasonable to think that it will contact others in similar situations. Most important, if it is indeed an extraordinarily good, wise, and powerful being, there is reason to think that intimate contact with it will be of great help in our efforts to lead good lives (just as such contact with a human being of exemplary character and wisdom would be likely to have such a result).[9] Further, for some religious experiences, all these expectations are fulfilled to a very high degree. (1) Many people have numerous "of-God" experiences and some even find themselves having a continual sense of the divine presence. (2) "Of-God" experiences are reported from almost every human culture, and the institutional traditions (e.g., churches) they sustain have been among the most enduring in human history. (3) In very many cases, those having "of-God" experiences undergo major moral transformations and find a purpose and strength of will they previously lacked.

It seems, then, that we can argue that religious experiences of God's presence do establish his existence. The experiences themselves give *prima facie* warrant to the claim that he exists, and the fulfillment of the expectations induced by the assumption that the experiences are veridical provides the further support needed for ultimate warrant. This form of an argument from religious experience could be impressively developed by employing detailed illustrations from the literature of religious experience. But here I want to proceed in a different direction, to examine the underpinnings of the argument by developing and discussing the major philosophical challenges to it.

2. Redescribing the Experiences

The most fundamental way of attacking the above appeal to direct perceptions of God is to question its assumption that the experiences referred to are in fact perceptual; i.e., that, as they occur, the experiences purport to be of an external divine object. There is no doubt that many say this is the nature of their experience and, similarly, no doubt that they have had something very impressive happen to them. But they could, after all, be misdescribing the subjective content of their own experience. And there might seem to be a very good reason for concluding that they are; namely, that there could, in principle, be no experiences of the sort they claim to have had. There are two ways of developing such an objection: (1) by trying to show that no experience could have the sort of object these experiences are said to have; (2) by trying to show that the alleged experiences of God are so different from our paradigmatic experiences of persons (namely, experiences of other humans) that they cannot be properly described as encounters with a person.

(1) There are some descriptions of God under which it might seem very odd to say that we had directly experienced him. How, for example, could we claim to have experienced him as the creator of the universe or as omniscient, omnipotent, and all-good? Surely, it might be thought, such attributes would have to be inferred from or read into an experience, not directly given in it. How, for

example, could an experience of the creator of the entire universe differ from one of the creator of everything except one planet? Or an experience of an all-loving being from an experience of a being who loved everything except Gallo Hearty Burgundy? Of course, the experiences we are concerned with are not typically claimed to be of God as creator, omnipotent, etc.; but they are claimed to be of someone encountered as far more powerful and good than any human being. How could even such lesser properties be given in an immediate experience? They might be inferrable from the nature of a person's interventions in the world, but not just from an awareness of a person's presence.

The assumption of the objections raised in the above paragraph is that some properties can be directly experienced by us whereas others cannot. This may well be true; but, if so, how do we know it? How, for example, do we know that we can ascertain the eye-color but not the total cash worth of a person by direct experience? One relevant consideration is whether experiencers can be reasonably thought to be in causal contact with states of affairs expressing the information they are said to know by direct experience. Thus, we might reject the claim that someone knows my total cash worth just by looking at me, on the grounds that the information is not available in my physical features or behavior. In the case of God, however, there is every reason to think that he can causally interact with anyone at any time. But given the causal accessibility of an object, surely the only way of knowing whether or not it can be experienced is to see if people actually do experience it. This, for example, is how most of us know that football referees' whistles, but not dog whistles, can be heard by human ears. There are no intrinsic characteristics of certain properties by which we can judge *a priori* that they can or cannot be directly perceived. Consequently, the assumption that divine qualities — even in the strong form of omnipotence, and the like — cannot be directly experienced could be justified only by showing that they are not experienced. Since this last claim is just what is at stake in discussions of religious experience, it is apparent that the present objection must beg the question.

(2) The second line of criticism has been interestingly developed by Ronald Hepburn.[10] He begins with the idea, put forward especially by Martin Buber and theologians influenced by him, that an encounter with God would have to be essentially different from our ordinary encounters with material things and even with human persons because all these encounters are with *objects* (*Its*), the presence of which can be checked for by the effects of their behavior in the world. For, according to this view:

> God . . . never becomes an *It*, an object: he is eternally a *Thou* only. There is no detecting *his* presence by bumps on the stair or even a whispered word or a glimpse of a face. We cannot, with *him*, point or glance in this or that direction and say, 'There, he is coming now.' We have only that felt sense of personal meeting, a sense of addressing and being addressed. He leaves no marks of his presence such that we might say — 'This proves he is with us' [*Christianity and Paradox*, p. 25].

The obvious question is, If an "encounter" with God is so different from our experience of objects, why even call it an experience of something? Because, it is said, we find in some of our experiences of human persons significant, though imperfect, analogies to an encounter with God. Specifically, it is possible to move from our ordinary, mundane encounters with other people, in which we regard them as little more than things equivalent to their behavioral effects in the world, to intimate experiences in which behavioral cues are of minimal significance and our apprehension of the other person becomes close to a direct *acquaintance* unmediated by knowledge of behavioral effects. Thus, we find in human relations degrees of "purity" of personal encounters, corresponding to a decreasing dependence of the encounters on behavioral cues.

From this, we can make sense of a totally pure "I-Thou" encounter with God.

Hepburn's objection to this view is that in fact it cannot make good on the claim that there are *any* encounters that even approach the ideal of a pure, unmediated awareness of personal presence. He considers several cases of human encounters, ranging from someone's studying my bodily movements in order to mimic them, to an intimate conversation, punctuated by long but pregnant pauses, with a close friend. Reflecting on these cases, he notes that in even the most intimate encounter it is entirely possible for me to be mistaken in my "sense" of the other's presence (e.g., I may still "sense" John's presence in the dark room where we have been speaking, even though he has slipped out during one of the pregnant pauses). Given this, Hepburn comments:

> The fact that we can make occasional mistakes about encounters with human beings . . . would not necessarily make nonsense of the scale of 'purity'. What *does* upset it is . . . the continuing importance of 'knowledge about' or 'knowledge that' in even the most intimate relationships. My ease of mind during John's silence is inductively justified by my memory of the countless times he has ended such a silence with words that showed he had been meditating on something I said to him. . . . The longer one has known somebody, the more experience one has gathered of him, the longer the gaps that one can allow between checking in various ways upon his reaction to what is being said and done. In *this* sense one is not so dependent on information *about* him. . . . But, again, this is so only because we assume consistency in our friend's personality. Whereas, the actual forms that his consistent behavior takes we have had to learn by watching, asking, and listening [pp. 35–36].

Hepburn's conclusion, accordingly, is that we have no ordinary analogues to the alleged "purely personal" encounter with God and so are not at all entitled to speak of these encounters as perceptual experiences.

However, even if Hepburn's assessment of "I-Thou" encounters with God is correct, his conclusion does not seem to apply to the sort of religious experience that concerns us. For the cases we have cited do not describe experiences of a person with no mediation via experiences of the person's activities. Rather, God is encountered as responding to the experiencer, aiding and comforting him, expressing his love. So these experiences meet Hepburn's condition that a perceptual experience of a person must involve an awareness of the person via "behavioral cues." Of course, the behavioral cues in this case are not sensorily perceived bodily states or activities. But to assume that the cues must be of this sort just begs the question by ruling out a priori the possibility of encountering nonembodied persons.

Further, Hepburn's argument does not even seem telling against a purported experience of a person unmediated by behavioral cues. For it is obvious that not everything we perceive is perceived mediately. In the case of our perception of human beings, for example, the behavior through which we perceive them is itself, in some cases, perceived directly, not by perceiving some further cue of the behavior. (Thus, I perceive Edward by hearing his words, but I do not hear his words by means of any further perception.) But, as we argued above, given the "causal availability" of a person, there is no a priori way of determining whether he can or cannot be directly perceived. Even if we know from experience that human persons cannot be directly perceived, it does not follow that the same is true of nonhuman persons. As noted above, the only way of finding out is to see what people have in fact perceived.

I suspect that Hepburn's real difficulty is not with the idea of directly perceiving a person, but with the claim that such a perception is self-authenticating and so cannot be checked by further experiences. Certainly, he sees the theologians he is criticizing as thinking that direct personal encounters with God are self-authenticating. Thus, in summarizing the view of H. H. Farmer, he says: "Encounter with God . . . is self-authenticating, 'known only through direct perception not describable in other terms'" (p. 40). But though this may be the view of Hepburn's opponents, there is no need to tie direct perception to self-authentification. After all, I may directly perceive that you have long blonde hair, and still revise my judgment when I see you removing a wig. Similarly, I might have a direct experience of God's presence and later rightly reject its veridicality on the grounds that it was drug-induced or had a negative moral effect on my life. It is true that in cases of direct perception *one* source of further checking is not available: we cannot ask if an error was made regarding the behavioral cues. But there can still be other sorts of checks, such as compatability with subsequent experiences.

I conclude, then, that attempts to redescribe presence-of-God experiences as nonperceptual are not successful.

3. Explaining the Experiences Away

When we are presented with the claim that a given religious experience is truly a revelation of the divine, we are often inclined to point out that the occurrence of the experience can be as well or better explained without the assumption that it was in fact produced by an encounter with God. Thus, we make reference to Freudian projections and wish fulfillments, group-induced expectations, schizophrenic personalities, and even the biochemistry of puberty to account for various religious experiences. Do such explanations truly impugn the veridicality of the experiences they try to account for? An adequate answer requires some reflection on the logic of explanation.

A first crucial point is that no explanation is acceptable unless there is reason to think that the explanandum it yields is true. There are no acceptable explanations of why there are only seven planets. Here there are two importantly different cases. In the first, the above condition is readily satisfied because we have good independent grounds for thinking that the premises of the explanation (the explanans) are true and so can conclude by a sound argument from them to the truth of the explanandum. In the second case, we do not have adequate independent support for the explanans, but rather hope that its successful explanation of the explanandum will help provide such support. In this case, we are justified in regarding the explanation as adequate only if we have good independent reason to think that the explanandum is true.

Let us now apply these comments to attempts to explain away the veridicality of an experience. To claim that an explanation of an experience shows that it is not veridical is to propose an explanans that yields an explanandum asserting the nonveridicality of the experience. The assertion will be justified only if there is reason to think the explanation is adequate, and this will be so only if there is reason to think the explanandum is true. In the first of the cases distinguished in the preceding paragraph, we can rightly regard the explanans itself as establishing the truth of the explanandum, and so the claim that the explanation has shown the nonveridicality of the experience is warranted. Thus, if we know on independent grounds that Jean-Paul has been taking mescaline and that taking mescaline usually causes him to have hallucinations of menacing crustaceans, then we have an explanation of his experience of menacing crustaceans that shows it to be nonveridical. But in the second case this conclusion may not be drawn. If we have no independent support for the claims of the explanans about Jean-Paul's drug use and its probable effects, then, in order to accept the explanation as adequate, we need to have independent support for the claim that Jean-Paul's experiences are nonveridical. In this case, then, the proposed explanation cannot be used to show that the experience it explains is nonveridical.

Our conclusion then must be that we can "explain away"

a religious experience only by means of an explanans whose truth we can establish independently of its purported explanatory power. With this in mind, let us examine some standard attempts to explain away religious experiences. It will be useful to distinguish two sorts of such attempts. The first are based on peculiarities of the individuals who have religious experiences; for example, it may be pointed out that a particular religious mystic shows signs of a psychosis that is typically associated with religious hallucinations. The second are based on traits common to everyone (or at least everyone belonging to some very broad class); thus, a Freudian might note that we all have unconscious desires to believe in the divine reality allegedly revealed in religious experiences.

The first sort of attempt to explain away religious experiences faces the initial difficulty of severe limitation in scope of application. Even if the "of-God" experiences of some people can be discounted because of their psychological abnormalities, the large number of apparently normal people reporting such experiences makes it extremely unlikely that such an approach could explain away all or even most of these experiences. The approach would be successful only if we had independent reason for thinking that the experiences were nonveridical and could then use this fact to support the hypothesis that there are hidden abnormalities in those who have them. But then, of course, the psychological explanation would presuppose rather than establish the nonveridicality of the experiences it explained.

Furthermore, it is not even clear that the independent establishment of an individual's psychological or physiological abnormalities would ordinarily impugn the veridicality of his religious experiences. The presence of psychotic traits or a history of use of hallucinatory drugs will often impugn the reliability of an individual's sense experiences, because we know that such conditions cause sensory distortions. But it is not so obvious that factors suggesting the unreliability of a person's sense experiences suggest a similar unreliability of his nonsensory experiences. *A priori,* there is just as much reason to think that the abnormalities that inhibit perceptions of material objects might enhance perception of nonmaterial objects.[11] Of course, we might discover correlations between certain psychological traits and the nonveridicality of the religious experiences of those who have them. But this would require some means, other than the appeal to psychological explanations, of determining the nonveridicality of religious experiences; and there is little likelihood that everyone reporting religious experiences would have the traits in question. So there is little reason to think that this first approach to explaining away religious experiences will be successful.

What about explanations of religious experiences on the basis of traits common to all human beings? Freud, for example, claims that "religious ideas . . . are fulfillments of the oldest, strongest and most urgent wishes of mankind." For example:

> . . . the benevolent rule of a divine Providence allays our fear of the dangers of life; the establishment of a moral world-order ensures the fulfillment of the demands of justice . . .; and the prolongation of earthly existence in a future life provides the local and temporal framework in which these wish-fulfillments shall take place.[12]

Given that we so deeply desire the truth of religious claims, it is not surprising that many people have experiences that seem to support their truth. For, as common sense suggests and depth psychology shows, there are mechanisms whereby the mind is capable, in certain circumstances, of seeing or otherwise experiencing what it wants to. Hence, from a Freudian perspective, there is a relatively straightforward explanation of religious experiences. Moreover, the premises of this explanation (that we desire religious claims to be true, that the mind can produce experiences fulfilling its wishes) have strong support apart from their role in explaining religious experiences. So shouldn't we conclude that this sort of account does undermine the veridicality of religious experiences?

No. The difficulty is this: even if we do have independent knowledge of the existence and the nature of the mechanisms of wish fulfillment, the Freudian explanation of any specific religious experience requires not only that these mechanisms exist as *capacities* but that they be actually operative in the occurrences of the experiences being explained. But there is no way of seeing the actual operation of wish-fulfillment mechanisms; we can only postulate them as the best explanation of the occurrence of delusory experiences. Hence, to be entitled to assert the actual operation of wish-fulfillment mechanisms, we must first have good reason to think that the experiences they explain are nonveridical. So the Freudian attempt to explain away religious experience is inevitably question-begging.

The same sort of difficulty faces Marxist explanations, based, for example, on the ideas that religious beliefs support the power of the ruling class and that there are socioeconomic forces capable of causing individuals to have experiences supporting these beliefs. We would need to know that these forces were in fact operative in a given case and to know this independent of information about the nonveridicality of the experiences. Similar strictures apply to any other attempts at general explanations (via social, economic, psychological or other causes) of religious experiences and beliefs. It is not sufficient to show just that such causes *could* produce the experiences and beliefs. It must also be shown that they are in fact operative in given cases; and it is very hard to see how this can be done without assuming ahead of time that the experiences and beliefs are nonveridical.

It is sometimes suggested — by both Freudians and Marxists — that *all* experiences are psychologically or economically determined. If we knew this to be so, then we would be justified in appealing to economic or psychological causes to explain religious experiences. It is hard to see what evidence could be put forward for these claims of universal determinism. But, given any such claim, we must surely allow that experiences can be veridical (and known to be so) in spite of their being determined, or else fall into an extreme skepticism. But then the mere fact that a religious experience is psychologically or economically determined does not undermine its veridicality.

A final difficulty facing Freudian and Marxist critiques of religious experience — and critiques based on any other general views of human reality and its place in the world — is that their own basic beliefs and the "evidence" they are said to be based on seem at least as susceptible to being explained away as are religious beliefs and experiences. There are after all Freudian explanations of Marxism and and Marxist explanations of Freudianism. (Not to mention the possibility of religious explanations of both.) The attempt to discredit general worldviews by proposing explanations themselves based on rival worldviews is a two-edged sword that can easily be turned against those who wield it.

So far we have been considering the possibility of showing religious experiences to be nonveridical by appealing to specific scientific (or purportedly scientific) theories that explain them. However, there is another way in which scientific explanation might seem to call religious experiences into question. Science, it might be argued, is ultimately our only source of reliable information about what there is. We begin, admittedly, with a commonsense view of the furniture of the universe, derived from our ordinary sense experience — the view Sellars calls "the manifest image." But this view is subject to correction and even ultimate replacement by the view of things — "the scientific image" — that results from the careful scrutiny of our world by the methods of postulational empirical science. To cite some standard examples, we have learned, contrary to manifest appearances, that color is not an intrinsic quality of external material objects, and that such objects are not homogeneous units but multitudinous aggregates of elementary particles. Of course science is far from having achieved a complete account of what there is; nonetheless, there is no basis for accepting the existence of entities and processes that show no sign of having a place in the ultimate scientific scheme of things. Nor is it just that immaterial agents such as God seem to have no place in this scheme. It also seems that the scientific study of the human mind and brain suggests no extrasensory faculties by which we might perceive such agents. From this point of view, the objection to religious experiences is not that they can be explained away by science but that there are no prospects for a positive scientific account of their veridicality. Since the view that these experiences are veridical finds no place in our scientific account of the world, it is reasonable to abandon it and to suppose that religious experiences are in fact the delusive products of one or another of the mechanisms capable of producing them.

Many religious believers will be inclined to simply dismiss this line of argument because of its apparently gratuitous assumption that science alone is capable of giving a complete account of what there is. In my opinion, such a dismissal ignores the very powerful case that can be made for a strong form of scientific realism.[13] In any case, it will not impress the nonbeliever who is committed to the primacy of science or even the believer who hesitates to make factual claims that go beyond or conflict with established scientific results. However, I do not think that the defense of religious experiences needs to reject the claims of scientific realism. We can both agree that "science is the measure of what there is" *and* claim that we have true encounters with God.

The reconciliation of scientific realism and religious experience depends, however, on a proper understanding of the import of realism. Realism is indeed a vain pretension if it claims that all truths are scientific truths and that nonscientific categories such as 'person', 'meaning', and 'good' must be either translated into scientific terms or else rejected as having no applications. Rather, such categories — and the truths expressed in their terms — must be regarded as valid and irreducible to science. Scientific realism is just the assertion that their validity does not derive from their reference to some special realm of entities that supplements those discovered by scientific inquiry.

This version of scientific realism has been brilliantly developed and defended by Wilfrid Sellars. He has, in particular, argued that an acceptance of realism does not require rejecting the framework of persons. Thus, at the end of his essay "Philosophy and the Scientific Image of Man,"[14] Sellars says:

> To say that a certain person desired to do A, thought it his duty to do B but was forced to do C, is not to *describe* him as one might describe a scientific specimen. One does indeed describe him, but one does something more. And it is this something more which is the irreducible core of the framework of persons [p. 39; Sellars's emphasis].

He goes on to suggest that this irreducible "something more" is the recognition of the person as belonging to a community with us: "Thus, to recognize a featherless biped or dolphin or Martian as a person is to think of oneself and it as belonging to a community" (ibid.). Sellars further argues that a community is defined by the most general *intentions* that are shared by its members. As a result, recognizing someone "as a person requires that one think thoughts of the form, 'We (one) shall do . . . actions of kind A in circumstances of kind C.'" Further, he emphasizes, "To think thoughts of this kind is not to *classify* or *explain,* but to rehearse an intention." Accordingly, he concludes:

> . . . the conceptual framework of persons is not something that needs to be *reconciled with* the scientific image, but rather something to be *joined* to it. Thus, to complete the scientific image

we need to enrich it *not* with more ways of saying what is the case, but with the language of community and individual intentions [p. 40; Sellars's emphasis].

Supposing that this approach to the framework of persons can be adequately developed (and Sellars has carried it a long way in various directions), we can accept a Sellarsian version of scientific realism and still maintain that there are irreducible truths about persons and their interrelations.

Sellars, of course, is concerned only with the framework of human persons. Does his account also allow for the recognition of a divine person? One apparent obstacle to such a recognition is this: Although the category of 'human person' is irreducible to scientific categories, the existence of truths about specific human persons depends on the existence of certain scientifically describable physical systems; namely, the scientific counterparts of what in the manifest image we call the person's body. Without such a system as the person's physical locus, talk of a person will lack the minimal ontological foothold it needs to be appropriate. Now it would seem that God is regarded as precisely a person who has no body and hence no physical locus, and so could not be countenanced by even Sellars's nonreductive scientific realism. However, it seems to me that orthodox religious thought allows and even suggests (by its claim that God is present everywhere in the world) the identification of the physical world as a whole as God's physical locus in the sense required by the Sellarsian account of persons. This is not pantheism: there is no suggestion that God is identical with his physical locus. Nor is there any need to accept a divine hylomorphism by thinking of God as having the world as his body in the sense that human beings have bodies. For though, like our bodies for us, the world is the vehicle whereby God communicates to human beings, there is no need to think that God's nature depends on the world the way that human nature depends on human bodies. Talk of the divine person could express truths that would hold regardless of the state of the physical world.

Another apparent difficulty: it might seem that, on the Sellarsian view, there could be truths about God only to the extent that we choose to recognize him as a person, by deciding to think of him and ourselves as members of a common community. But it is just as possible that the community in which God has his reality as a person exists most fundamentally in virtue of *his* intentions toward us, not vice versa (just as infants are included in the human community in virtue of the intentions of adults).

A final objection: Won't the Sellarsian view at least entail that God cannot exist if the universe does not, and so be inconsistent with God's autonomy and role as creator of all that is? For even Sellars's realism cannot admit the existence of a person with no physical locus, since this would mean that there was a reality in no way accessible to scientific discovery. Here I think a certain retreat from the strict realist ontological view might be necessary, but it is not a retreat that rejects the central insights that motivate realism. Realism, as I am considering it, is essentially a claim about the methods of inquiry whereby we can arrive at a true account of reality. It holds that scientific methods of inquiry are the only ones that we can rely on to produce a complete and accurate account of what there is. If, however, as religious experiences suggest, the world is the physical locus of a divine person with whom we have direct perceptual contact, there arises the possibility of obtaining information about what there is from this person. Such information could not contradict what we do or could know by pursuit of scientific inquiry. But it could supplement what is so known; for example, by telling us that the divine person exists in essential independence of the physical universe. Our coming to know this would refute a realist claim that we can have no knowledge of what there is apart from science. But since the knowledge would have been given to us by authoritative revelation and not obtained by any human methods of inquiry, it would be consistent with the essential realist view that there are no methods except those of science whereby we can, *on our own authority,* rightly assert anything about what there is.

4. Religious Experiences and Religion

So far the objections we have considered have derived from epistemological considerations quite separate from, if not opposed to, the content of religious beliefs. In this section we turn to objections derived from religion itself. I will first examine the suggestion that the true God's transcendence and utter uniqueness make it impossible for him to be the object of a human experience (at least of the relatively straightforward perceptual experiences with which we are concerned).

More precisely, the difficulty can be formulated in this way: any object given in our experience must be properly characterizable in terms of our concepts. (On a Kantian view, the experience is possible only if the object is given under our concepts; on an empiricist view, we could abstract the concepts from the object as experienced.) But it is an essential feature of God that none of our concepts are properly applicable to him.[15] For, if they were, he would be just another thing in our world, even if a preeminent one, and not the creator of this world. So, if a being is given as an object of our experience, one thing we can surely conclude is that it is not the God who created us and whom we worship. We may, on this view, allow for special "mystical experiences" that are not encounters with an external object but rapturous unions with God that, as the mystics insist, cannot be described in human language and concepts. But these are very different from the perceptions of God that are our focus here. Indeed, to the extent that mystical experiences are accepted as true manifestations of God, they show that our more mundane perceptions of a powerful and good person are not.

There are at least three important lines of response to this difficulty. First, it should be noted that the objection does not in fact question the veridicality of experiences of a good and powerful person concerned about us. At best, it shows that there is another religiously relevant being, not encountered in these experiences. If it is true that this unexperienceable being is the primary focus of religious belief, then our "of-God" experiences do not ground the central claim of religion. Nonetheless, the existence of the sort of being revealed in these experiences must be of very great importance for us. Second, even religious views that most emphasize the utter transcendence of God (e.g., some versions of Christianity and Hinduism) allow for the role of mediators (angels, lesser gods) between God and man. So even if our experiences are not strictly of God, they may still be important factors in our relation to him. Finally, there is the possibility – at the heart of Christianity in the doctrine of incarnation – that even a transcendent God might reveal himself to us by taking on a human form. Christians who hold that a man living among us was the transcendent God can hardly reject the possibility that this God could reveal himself to us in nonsensory experiences. This possibility is further supported by the fact that, even if none of our concepts are properly applicable to God, there must be some that are more adequate than others to his reality. Thus, it is surely less of a mistake to say that God is good and powerful than to say that he is neurotic and deciduous. But if this is so, there would seem to be room for an experience – although imperfect – of God in terms of the concepts most appropriate to him.

Another objection drawn from religion is based on the alleged wide diversity in the content of experiences of God and the apparent dependence of this content on the religious traditions of the experiencers. This diversity is undeniable if we take account of the entire range of religious experiences; but it is by far most prominent in the extreme cases of literal visions and the "private revelations" of the most advanced mystics. The Virgin Mary does not appear to Hindus; Moslems do not have mystical encounters with the Trinity. But at best this sort of diversity shows that religious experience does not establish the superiority of one religious tradition over others. The fact remains that in all traditions there are countless experiences of a superhuman loving power concerned about us; and even the otherwise divergent physical and mystical visions share this essential core of content.

There are, it is true, two crucial questions on which there are differences between and even within traditions: Is the divine reality truly other than that of the experiencer? And is the divine reality personal or impersonal? However, the difference between those who answer these questions affirmatively and those who answer them negatively is not so great as it might seem. Even those who emphasize the unity of God and self admit that God is other than the ordinary mundane self of our everyday life. So in spite of their insistence that there is an ultimate unity, they agree that the divine is other than the "finite" or "illusory" self that is transcended in rapturous union with the divine. Given this, they could surely also admit the possibility of an essentially veridical, although incomplete, encounter of the finite self with God. Similarly, those who encounter God as "impersonal" do not claim that he is more like a rock than a human being, but that even the category of 'person' is not adequate to his reality. Even so, there is no reason that an encounter with God as a person could not be partially revelatory of the divine nature or perhaps an experience of a mediator between us and God. So, despite the manifest diversity of religious experiences, there remains a content common to them all; and, apart from very uncommon instances of highly specific revelations via visions or mystical insights, it is possible to accept consistently the essential features of almost all religious experiences.

5. Religious Experiences and the Justification of Religious Belief

People candidly report that they have directly experienced the presence of a good and powerful nonhuman being concerned about us. The experiences are not isolated events in their lives but are followed by other and more intimate encounters with this being, sometimes even to the point of an abiding sense of its presence. These encounters are a source of moral strength and comfort, even more than we would expect from prolonged and intimate contact with the most admirable human. Further, similar experiences with similar effects are reported by great numbers of people from diverse times and places. There is no reason to think that these experiences do not have the perceptual character attributed to them, and there are no explanations of them (as a whole) as delusory that are not question-begging. Further, there are few if any other religious experiences that contradict their central content. Surely, we then have very good reason to believe that at least some of these experiences are veridical and hence that there is a good and powerful being, concerned about us, who has revealed himself to human beings. So much, I think, is established by our discussion so far.

To what extent does this conclusion justify religious belief? If we have in mind the beliefs of the great majority of religious people, the answer is: very little. Typically, religious belief includes substantive accounts of the nature of God (e.g., that he is omnipotent, omniscient, all-good, the creator of all things, triune, etc.), of his relations to man (e.g., that he became man to save us, that this salvation is carried out by sacramental acts within specific religious communities), of the moral ideals (self-sacrifice, love for all men) that should animate our lives, and of an after-life dependent on the moral quality of our lives here on earth. Hardly anything of any such accounts is justified by knowing that there is a powerful and good being concerned about us. We can sum up the situation by saying that "of-God" experiences provide us much more with *access to* than with *accounts of* God. Of course, this access neces-sarily involves some minimal description of what is en-countered, but this description falls far short of what is asserted by any major religion and of what is held by almost all believers.

However, these experiences still have very great signifi-cance. First and most importantly, they establish the crucial claim that religion as a pervasive phenomenon of human life is based on a genuine contact with a reality be-yond ourselves. As C. D. Broad said after a characteristically judicious assessment of the veridicality of religious ex-periences:

> The claim of any particular religion or sect to have complete or final truth on these subjects seems to me to be too ridiculous to be worth a moment's consideration. But the opposite extreme of holding that the whole religious experience of mankind is a gigan-tic system of pure delusion seems to me to be almost (though not quite) as farfetched.[16]

Further, the fact that the religious beliefs of mankind derive to at least some extent from an access to the divine warrants our taking seriously the major beliefs of the great world religions. These beliefs have been formed (in part at least) by the sustained and intimate contact of generations of people with a superhuman power; and so, even if they are not to be believed without question, they ought to be carefully and respectfully scrutinized as potential sources of truth. Finally, given the fact that the great world reli-gions seem to be the main loci and sustainers of our access to God, there is good reason for anyone interested in at-taining such access or in more deeply understanding what it reveals to take part in the life of some established religious community. (And to these considerations many can add the happiness and moral inspiration they find in the fellowship of a particular religious tradition.)

So it seems that accepting the veridicality of religious experiences can provide good reasons for associating ourselves with the great religious traditions of mankind. There is no *a priori* reason why this association must be with one particular tradition or even a specific church. But for many people there will be specific psychological and social factors that make their participation in just one tradition or church most valuable. Moreover, the richness and diversity of the religious life of any one major tradition suggests that most of us will lose little by so restricting our primary commitment. On the contrary, a refusal to participate fully in some specific "form of religious life" may lead to an abstract and superficial religiosity that will fall far short of profiting from what the religious experiences of humankind have to offer. So, for many people at least, there is good reason for a commitment to a particular religious community.

But there is a serious question about the nature of this commitment. If my participation in the life of a religious community is not to be hypocritical, I surely must share the *beliefs* on which this life is based. But, since hardly any of these beliefs are justified by the appeal to religious experience (or, it would seem, by any other standard apologetic arguments), how can I in all honesty accept them?

One possible approach here is an appeal to a version of the pragmatic defense of religious belief. I know that great personal benefits are available to me if I participate fully in the life of a specific religious community, and that this full participation requires sharing the beliefs of this community. So, for the sake of the benefits, I am entitled to hold certain beliefs even though I have no reasons supporting their truth. This will be a sound argument, supposing that the benefits of believing can in fact be shown to take precedence over the epistemic value (or even obligation) of guiding belief by evidence. But even if sound, such a pragmatic argument represents an unfortunate need to subordinate our search for *knowledge* (i.e., belief justified by reasons relevant to the truth of what is believed) to other values. And there is the very real possibility (supported by Nietzsche's critique of religious belief) that the soundness of the pragmatic argument derives from the weakness of those for whom it applies. For isn't the argument based on the idea that our happiness requires the crutch of beliefs not known to be true, and wouldn't stronger psyches be able to thrive merely on what they can show to be true?

This challenge can be met by considerations similar to those put forward in our discussion (in chapter 3) of the principle of methodological conservatism. Specifically, we can invoke the Millian argument that the interests of truth itself are best served by debates between those who are genuinely committed to opposing views. Our best chance of eventually reaching the truth about questions to which different religions give different answers is to see to it that there are continuing discussions of these questions, and that at least some of those taking part in the discussions defend with all their resources beliefs they themselves hold. In this way, the pragmatic justification for a commitment to a specific set of religious beliefs can be shown to be entirely in accord with our epistemic obligation to further the search for truth based on evidence.

However, this defense of a specific set of religious beliefs has the same limitations as a defense of beliefs by appeal to methodological conservatism: it warrants only interim, not decisive, assent to the beliefs in question. That is, they are rightly assented to, but only with the understanding that there is epistemic need for continuing discussion of their truth status. As I argued earlier, a merely interim assent is not sufficient for the sort of commitment that seems to be involved in religious belief. However, the decisive assent needed for such a commitment is appropriate to the belief, warranted by religious experience, in the existence of a divine being as the object of that experience. Accordingly, it seems to me that we must make an important distinction between two aspects of religious belief. First, there is what we might call a "core" of belief to which decisive assent is given. Such assent should not be given to any substantive account of the details of God's nature and his relations with us (such as those offered by the creeds and theologies of religions), but only to the reality of a superhuman power and love in our lives, as this has been revealed by religious experiences of the presence of God. Second, there is an "outer belt" of belief (similar to what James calls "overbelief") to which only interim assent is appropriate.[17] Here are included almost all the content of the creeds and theologies that express the distinctive commitments of specific religions.

This distinction of a core and an outer belt of belief makes good sense of the idea, often put forward by believers, that their faith is not so much a matter of believing that certain propositions are true as it is of believing in a person. Of course, belief in a person does require belief that the person exists and has a basic set of identifying properties. But the core of religious faith has only a very minimal propositional content, and consists primarily of living with an awareness of and an openness to the power and goodness of a divinity that remains essentially mysterious to us. The greatest cognitive failure of religions throughout history has been their confusion, due to a fundamental self-misunderstanding, of the core and the outer belt of their commitment. This confusion leads to demands for decisive assent to claims that at best deserve interim assent. These demands are rightly rejected as intellectually irresponsible, with the result that religion is regarded as a thoroughly unreasonable commitment. The separation of a core of belief from the outer belt of overbelief provides the basis for a rehabilitation of the cognitive claims of religion.

We should not, however, fall into the opposite error of thinking that what I have called the outer belt is an unimportant part of religious belief. As we have already noted, such beliefs do originate from sustained and intimate contacts with God, and so at least point in the direction of important truths. We have also seen that a commitment to them is an integral part of full participation in the life of religious communities. Moreover, the outer belt is relevant to the justification of the core of religious belief. The reason is that the appeal to religious experiences of the divine will be (rightly) rejected out of hand if there are no coherent and intelligible ways of including a divine reality in our best available accounts of man and his world. If, for example, the only way we had today of thinking of the divine were in terms of a literal understanding of the ancient Greek or Norse myths, then we would have every reason to reject the veridicality of religious experiences on the grounds that there is independent reason to think that their purported objects do not exist. Consequently, the viability of the core of religious belief requires that the idea of a divine reality be formulated in ways that show it to be a significant possibility in terms of our best available general accounts of reality. Such formulations maintain religious belief as a "live option" in the general cultural context in which the believer lives. They do not themselves justify the core of belief, but they make essential intellectual room for beliefs based on religious experience. The detailed doctrinal formulations (inevitably carried out in terms of available secular intellectual resources) that I have called the "outer belt" of religious belief perform just this function. They make the idea of a divine presence in the world the central assertion of a comprehensive and detailed account of man and his world. This account goes far beyond what is justified by our experiences of the divine; but, properly developed, it should present an intellectually respectable worldview when judged in the context of our best secular accounts. In this way the outer belt plays an essential role in the justification of religious belief.

Conclusion

At the outset of this book, I suggested that my discussion would dissolve the standard dichotomy between religious faith and skepticism. We can now see how this suggestion has been confirmed. On the side of faith, I have argued for the existence of a divine person: a good and powerful being, concerned about us, who is encountered in religious experiences. Further, I have identified traditional religions as the primary loci of contact with this being and argued for the right of believers to endorse the accounts of God and his relations to us that are given by their religions. To this extent, I find the claims of faith rationally well founded. Nevertheless, my position remains skeptical in very important respects. The assertion that there is a good and powerful being concerned about us is the *only* religious claim that I see as worthy of the decisive assent that is essential to religious belief as traditionally construed. (And it is at least not entirely clear that the God who is the object of this assent is the omniperfect God of traditional religions.) Although I think we can be entitled to religious beliefs beyond this core, I see no irrationality in withholding such beliefs (indeed, it can be entirely rational to deny them) and no justification for more than an interim assent to them. Since traditional religious views require decisive assent to numerous truths beyond that included in my core, it is fair to say that I reject these views. In this sense, I am skeptical about religion.

Nevertheless, it is more accurate to describe my view as both skeptical and religious. I have said that I see religions as giving us reliable access to a divine being, but not reliable accounts of him. They are the primary loci and instruments of encounters with God; but their doctrinal accounts of his nature and relations to us, though worthy of respect, cannot be justifiably given decisive assent. The primary self-misunderstanding of religions has been to think of themselves as repositories of ultimate truth, rather than as wavering pointers to an ultimate mystery. Rather than telling us what we want to know – the final meaning of our lives – religions tell us just enough about a world beyond but crucially related to ours to make us realize that no overall account we are able to give of our situation is adequate. If an account omits the divine reality, it is surely questionable; but so are accounts of this reality, since we know almost nothing of God beyond his presence to us. As a result, a primary function of religion – particularly in a world so full as ours of both secular and religious messiahs – is a skeptical one: to remind us that all our attempts to grasp the essential truth and meaning of our lives are mere guesses that we have no reason for trusting.

The pretensions of all ideologies – scientific, political, aesthetic, ethical and religious – are discredited by the simple truths that God is present to our world and that we are ignorant of the ultimate significance of that presence. If there were no reason to think there is a God in contact with us, one or another secular worldview (liberalism, Marxism, existentialism) might be able to establish itself as the truth for man. If we knew enough about God and his relations to us, we might find in one or another of the world's religions the ultimate meaning of our lives. As it is, we know just enough to call into question all claims to have discoverd any such meaning. We are, accordingly, left with the few particular truths and values we have been able to discover, without knowing how, if at all, they fit into some overall picture of our destiny. My final faith is that these fragments are enough.

Notes

Notes to Chapter 1

1. I should emphasize at the outset that my discussion of Wittgenstein's *Lectures* is not intended as an interpretation of his overall view but as a starting point for my own reflections about religious belief. Indeed, what we have in the *Lectures* is too fragmentary and opaque to support any such interpretation or to show with certainty that Wittgenstein held some definite view of religion. For a similar caution, see W. D. Hudson's comments at the outset of his helpful discussion of the *Lectures* in *Wittgenstein and Religious Belief* (New York: Macmillan, 1975).

2. *Lectures and Conversations on Aesthetics, Psychology, and Religious Belief*, ed. C. Barrett (Oxford: Blackwell, 1966), p. 53. Further references to this volume will be given in the body of the text.

3. Wilfrid Sellars, "Some Reflections on Langauge-Games," in *Science, Perception, and Reality* (London: Routledge & Kegan Paul, 1963), ch. 11.

4. Wittgenstein's discussion of the role of pictures in religion is very suggestive and worth pursuing. W. D. Hudson offers a good start along this line in *Wittgenstein and Religious Belief*, pp. 162–167; 171–75.

5. Sellars emphasizes that in speaking of the *rules* of a language-game we are not committed to the view that participants in the game have "the intention of fulfilling the demands of an envisaged system of rules" ("Some Reflections on Language-Games," p. 325). Typically speakers neither obey explicitly formulated rules nor merely conform to them (in the manner of empirical regularities). Rather, their

behavior is "pattern-governed" by the structures of the language-game in which they participate. The rules express these structures. Speakers act as they do *because of* the rules (i.e., we can explain their behavior by noting that they are playing the game and pointing out certain rules of the game); but they do not act with the intention of fitting their behavior to rules (see p. 329).

6. *On Certainty,* eds. G. E. M. Anscombe and G. H. von Wright, trans. Denis Paul and G. E. M. Anscombe (New York: Harper & Row, 1972), par. 250.

7. Ibid., par. 111.

8. Ibid., par. 1.

9. Norman Malcolm, "The Groundlessness of Belief," in S. Brown, ed., *Reason and Religion* (Ithaca, N.Y.: Cornell University Press, 1977), p. 146. Further references to this article will be given in the text.

10. Kai Nielsen has made this point very effectively in his "Wittgensteinian Fideism" (*Philosophy,* 1967, pp. 191–209) and a number of later essays in which he attacks the "compartmentalization" of religion.

11. Peter Winch, "Understanding a Primitive Society," in Steven M. Cahn, ed., *Philosophy of Religion* (New York: Harper & Row, 1970), p. 84.

12. Ibid., p. 103.

13. D. Z. Phillips, "Religious Beliefs and Language-Games," ch. 5 of *Faith and Philosophical Inquiry* (London: Routledge & Kegan Paul, 1970), pp. 101–2. The next three quotations are also from this essay.

14. D. Z. Phillips, *Death and Immortality* (London: Macmillan, 1970), pp. 44–45. The next three quotations are also from this work.

15. Ibid., p. 54; *Phaedo,* 64a.

16. Ibid., p. 49; *Tractatus,* 6.4312.

17. See D. Z. Phillips, "Belief, Change, and Forms of Life: The Confusions of Internalism and Externalism," in Frederick Crosson, ed., *The Autonomy of Religious Belief* (Notre Dame, Ind.: University of Notre Dame Press, 1981), pp. 60–92.

18. Ibid., p. 62.

19. W. D. Hudson has also emphasized the need to ground the Wittgensteinian thesis in an account of talk about God: "To substantiate this contention [that "attempts to make sense of religion,

or to validate its claims, in non-religious terms are self-defeating"] we must show that the grammar of religious belief is such that the object with which it has to do is ultimately different from that with which other universes of discourse have to do. God is not a physical thing, not a moral obligation, not an aesthetic emotion, not anything other than God." (*Wittgenstein and Religious Belief*, p. 157).

20. D. Z. Phillips, *The Concept of Prayer* (London: Routledge & Kegan Paul, 1965), pp. 13-14; Phillips' emphasis.

21. Ibid., p. 102.

22. I. Lakatos and A. Musgrave, eds., *Criticism and the Growth of Knowledge* (New York: Cambridge University Press, 1970), p. 101.

23. *The Concept of Prayer*, p. 19.

24. Norman Malcolm, "Anselm's Ontological Argument," *Philosophical Review*, 1960, p. 60.

Notes to Chapter 2

1. Alvin Plantinga, *Does God Have a Nature?* (Milwaukee: Marquette University Press, 1980), pp. 22-23.

2. David Burrell, *Exercises in Religious Understanding* (Notre Dame, Ind.: University of Notre Dame Press, 1974), ch. 3. Further references to this volume will be given in the text. See also the same author's treatment of this topic in *Aquinas: God and Action* (Notre Dame, Ind.: University of Notre Dame Press, 1979). These two discussions have some differences of emphasis and terminology, but they give essentially the same account. I have followed the earlier discussion because of its greater detail on the key notion of experiential intimations of God's reality.

3. Timothy McDermott, ed., *Summa Theologiae*, Vol. II: *Existence and Nature of God* (New York: McGraw-Hill, 1964), p. 18, editor's note a; cited by Burrell, *Exercises*, p. 86.

4. Here I state the formula as Burrell states it in his *Aquinas*. In *Exercises in Religious Understanding* he employs the simpler form, "to be God is to be"; but in the later book he insists the latter is "only a shorthand summary and that the longer formula is a must . . . for purposes of analysis" (p. 186, n. 1).

5. See Alvin Plantinga, *The Nature of Necessity* (Oxford: Clarendon Press, 1974), ch. 10.

6. For a detailed critique of the five ways along the lines sketched here, see Victor Preller, *Divine Science and the Science of God* (Princeton, N.J.: Princeton University Press, 1967), ch. 3.

7. In Aquinas' first way, for example, he does not justify his claim that there must be a first in the series of movers. He argues that other movers move only insofar as they are moved by the first mover, but this just assumes the point at issue.

Notes to Chapter 3

1. "The Reformed Objection to Natural Theology," *Proceedings of the American Catholic Philosophical Association,* 1980. Page references to this article will be given in the text.

2. The alternative to foundationalism is a coherentism that would require the justification of *every* belief in a rational noetic structure by its coherence with the totality of the structure's beliefs. On such a view Plantinga's suggestion that religious beliefs need no justification is excluded from the outset. (But the project of justifying religious belief becomes much easier to carry out.)

3. On the distinction of strong and weak foundationalism, see William Alston, "Two Types of Foundationalism," *Journal of Philosophy,* 1979.

4. His main objection is that formulations of classical foundationalism seem to be inevitably self-referentially incoherent. Specifically, their criteria of basicality are neither themselves basic nor derivable from basic propositions. Plantinga's critique of classical foundationalism is developed in "Is Belief in God Rational?", in C. F. Delaney, ed., *Rationality and Religious Belief* (Notre Dame, Ind.: University of Notre Dame Press, 1979).

5. I will speak of the principle of methodological conservatism as *justifying* beliefs because Goldstick and Sklar discuss it as a principle of justification. As will be apparent, the sort of justification the principle provides is not of the ordinary sort; and it is probably better to think of the principle as describing a situation in which we are entitled to take a proposition as basic. I will, however, keep the terminology that has been established in previous discussions.

6. "Methodological Conservatism," *American Philosophical Quarterly,* 1971. Page references will be given in the text.

7. "Methodological Conservatism," *Philosophical Review*, 1975. Page references will be given in the text.

8. It might seem that my formulation of the principle is self-contradictory, since it says both that *p* is epistemically indeterminate for A and that A is entitled to believe *p*. But *p*'s being epistemically indeterminate entails only that A is not entitled to believe it *on the basis of evidence for its truth*. There may be other, truth-independent considerations that entitle A to believe *p*. See my comments below (p. 103) on the distinction between reasons for the truth of *p* and reasons for believing the truth of *p*.

9. *Confessions*, X, 27.38-28.39; translation from *Fathers of the Church* (Washington, D.C.: Catholic University of America Press, 1948-62), p. 297.

Notes to Chapter 4

1. Basil Mitchell, *The Justification of Religious Belief* (New York: Seabury, 1973). All page references will be given in the text.

2. Thomas Kuhn, *The Structure of Scientific Revolutions*, 2nd ed. (Chicago: University of Chicago Press, 1969).

3. "Reflections on My Critics," in Lakatos and Musgrave, eds., *Criticism and the Growth of Knowledge* (New York: Cambridge University Press, 1970), p. 262.

4. Ian Barbour, *Myths, Models, and Paradigms* (New York: Harper & Row, 1974). All page references will be given in the text.

5. *The Structure of Scientific Revolutions*, p. x.

6. Ibid., p. 149.

7. Ibid., p. 151.

8. Ibid., p. 169.

9. For a fuller development of this interpretation of Kuhn, see my "Introduction" to Gary Gutting (ed.), *Paradigms and Revolutions: Applications and Appraisals of Thomas Kuhn's Philosophy of Science* (Notre Dame: University of Notre Dame Press, 1980).

10. For example, the theist often suggests that God may have failed to intervene to prevent an evil that we would feel bound to prevent because he saw that it was better for some creature to decide freely whether or not to prevent the evil, even though the creature's decision was not to intervene. Here the claim is that, for example,

the devil's exercise of freedom is of greater value, on the whole, than the child's life. This may be so, but it surely does not seem to be so from our point of view. Therefore, the theist has no alternative to appealing to the inscrutability of God's purpose, an inscrutability deriving not from God's peculiar moral framework but from his maximal knowledge of facts relevant to moral decisions. I should emphasize that my suggestion is that the believer has to endorse this sort of divine inscrutability to *explain* the existence of certain evils; he need not endorse it to show the *consistency* of God's existence with the existence of evil (as is done in the free will defense) since this requires only the claim that the inscrutability is logically possible. The believer, it seems to me, must endorse the inscrutability of God's ways only if he goes beyond a defense to the explanatory project of a theodicy. (On the distinction of defense and theodicy, see A. Plantinga, *The Nature of Necessity* [Oxford: Clarendon Press, 1974], p. 192.)

11. Jorge-Luis Borges, *A Personal Anthology* (New York: Grove Press, 1967), p. 80.

12. These are the criteria proposed by Kuhn in his paper "Objectivity, Value Judgment, and Theory Choice" in *The Essential Tension* (Chicago: University of Chicago Press, 1977).

13. Ibid., p. 322.

14. Richard Swinburne, *The Existence of God* (New York: Oxford University Press, 1979), p. 289.

15. Ibid., p. 291.

Notes to Chapter 5

1. W. James, *The Varieties of Religious Experience* (New York: Mentor Books, 1958; originally published 1902). Page references are given in the text.

2. D. Hay, "Religious Experience Amongst a Group of Post-Graduate Students — A Qualitative Study," *Journal for the Scientific Study of Religion* 18 (1979) pp. 164–82.

3. "Visions," in A. Flew and A. MacIntyre, eds., *New Essays in Philosophical Theology* (London: Macmillan, 1955), pp. 254–55.

4. W. Matson, *The Existence of God* (Ithaca, N.Y.: Cornell University Press, 1965).

5. A. Flew, *God and Philosophy* (New York: Harcourt, Brace & World, 1966), p. 129.

6. R. Swinburne, *The Existence of God* (New York: Oxford University Press, 1979). References will be given in the text.

7. I am saying in effect that there is inductive basis for applying the Principle of Credulity to ordinary experiences but not to religious ones. Swinburne considers this suggestion but rejects it on the following grounds:

> . . . an induction from past experiences to future experiences is only reliable if we correctly recall our past experiences. And what grounds do we have for supposing that we do? Clearly not inductive grounds — an inductive justification of the reliability of memory claims would obviously be circular. Here clearly we must rely on the principle that things are the way they seem as a basic principle not further justifiable. . . . And if it is justifiable to use [this principle] when other justifications fail in memory cases, what good argument can be given against using it in other kinds of cases when other justifications fail? (*The Existence of God*, p. 256).

But in fact it is not clear that memory claims admit of no justification apart from an appeal to the Principle of Credulity. A memory claim might, for example, be supported by its coherence with an immense body of other memory claims and present experiences; or it might be properly regarded as basic. Neither of these moves is appropriate to support the veridicality of religious experiences.

8. C. B. Martin, "A Religious Way of Knowing," in A. Flew and A. MacIntyre, eds., *New Essays in Philosophical Theology* (London: Macmillan, 1955). Page references will be given in the text.

9. All the expectations mentioned presuppose that the being encountered in religious experience would act in ways that we would (or should) in similar circumstances. Therefore, for the reasons suggested in ch. 4, there can be no support from the fulfillment of these expectations for the omniscience of the being encountered (because we would not expect an omniscient being to act as we would, with our very limited knowledge). If, however, the experience has been of the being as omniscient and other aspects of the experience are corroborated, then some support is provided for the claim that the being is omniscient, because there is support for the overall reliability of the experience. Further, an experience of a being as omniscient would be corroborated by subsequent experiences of its great knowledge (e.g., by its predicting unexpected events or revealing

profound truths about human nature that we were unlikely to have discovered ourselves). Similarly, experiences of a being as omnipotent and all-good can be corroborated by subsequent experiences of its power and benevolence. It seems, however, that most presence-of-God experiences present him simply as very wise, powerful, and good, and do not support strict doctrines of omniscience, omnipotence, and omnibenevolence. If so, these doctrines belong to what I will call the "outer belt" of belief, not to its "core."

10. R. Hepburn, *Christianity and Paradox* (London: C. A. Watts & Co., 1958). Page references will be given in the text.

11. C. B. Broad makes this point in *Religion, Philosophy and Psychical Research* (London: Routledge & Kegan Paul, 1953), p. 198.

12. Sigmund Freud, *The Future of an Illusion* (Garden City, N.Y.: Doubleday, 1964), pp. 47–48.

13. For a defense of scientific realism, see my paper "Scientific Realism," in J. C. Pitt, ed., *The Philosophy of Wilfrid Sellars: Queries and Extensions* (Dordrecht: Reidel, 1978).

14. Wilfrid Sellars, *Science, Perception, and Reality* (New York: Humanities Press, 1963). Page references will be given in the text.

15. As noted at the beginning of ch. 2, the literal claim that none of our concepts apply to God is absurd. Someone defending the view discussed in the text would have to formulate it on the basis of the thesis that anything we experience must properly (e.g., literally) fall under our concepts. When this modification is made, the thesis is at least not obviously true.

16. Broad, op. cit., pp. 200–201.

17. The terms "core" and "outer belt" are adapted from Lakatos's philosophy of science, which distinguishes the "hard core" and "protective belt" of scientific research programs ("The Methodology of Scientific Research Programmes," in I. Lakatos and A. Musgrave, eds., *Criticism and the Growth of Knowledge* [New York: Cambridge University Press, 1970]). The meaning I have given the terms is similar to, but by no means essentially the same as, that given them by Lakatos.

Index

Alston, William, 184
Analogical language, 52, 54–55, 62
Aquinas, St. Thomas, 49, 52, 139
  and proofs of God's existence, 65–77
  on talk about God, 53–65
Arguments, for God's existence, 44–49
  causal, 69–75
  cumulative case, 127–40
  from miracles, 69–70
  from religious experience, 66–67, ch. 5
  ontological, 46–48, 65–66
  the five ways, 73–75
Augustine, St., 106–7
Assent, interim vs. decisive, 4, 105–8, 174–75
Azande, 33–34, 77

Barbour, Ian, 112–13, 118–22
Basic statements, 80–83
Belief
  believing p equivalent to believing p is true, 103
  an act rather than an action, 102–3
  epistemically indeterminate, 100
  religious, see Religious belief
Borges, Jorge-Luis, 130
Broad, C.D., 172
Burrell, David, 49, 52, 53–65, 71, 73, 76

Calvin, John, 84
Concepts, religious 18–22

Disagreement about religion
  and Kuhnian paradigms, 124–25
  and the proper basicality of belief, 83–92
  contradiction model of, 15ff
  Wittgenstein on, 15–24

Egoism, epistemological, 86ff
Enlightenment, the, 11
Evil, problem of, 126, 130

Explanation
    causal, in science and in nat-
        ural theology, 67–69, 72–
        73
    explanatory power of theism,
        73–75, 127–40
    logic of, in causal arguments,
        71–73
    of miracles, 69–70
    of religious experiences, 158–
        63

Faith, vs. knowledge, 105
Flew, Anthony, 5, 146–47
Forms of life, religions as, 77–
    78, 173
Foundationalism, 31, 80–83
    weak vs. strong, 80–81
Framework principles and reli-
    gious belief, 29–32, 43,
    134
Freud, Sigmund, 161

God
    access to vs. accounts of, 172
    arguments for the existence
        of, see Arguments, for
        God's existence
    as (first) cause, 45–46, 57–
        58, 67–69, 70–76
    consistency of the concept
        of, 47–48
    essence and existence identi-
        cal in, 56ff
    experienceability of, 63–64,
        66–67, 153–58, 168–71
    incomprehensibility of, 50–52
    langauge about, 50–65
    nature of, 56–65

necessity of, 44–48
omniscience of, 129–30, 187
Goldstick, D., 92–96
Gutting, Gary, 185, 188

Hay, D., 186
Hepburn, Ronald, 155–58
Hudson, W.D., 181, 182–83

Immortality, 37–40
Interpretation, internal vs.
    external, 21

James, William, 141–43
Justification of religious belief
    by judgment vs. by proof, 76
    nature of, 5–8
    need for, Chapter 1, 50–52,
        65–78
    pragmatic, 91, 101–2, 173–74
    truth-oriented vs. truth-
        independent, 91–92, 96,
        102–3, 109
    vs. defense, 41–42

Kierkegaard, S., 37
Kuhn, Thomas, 112–13, 116–27

Lakatos, I., 45, 104, 188
Language games
    internalism vs. externalism,
        40–42, 43
    moves within vs. entry- and
        exit-transitions, 17ff, 59ff
    systems of religious beliefs as,
        16ff

Language, religious, 16ff, 44–49, 53–65
  autonomy of, 32ff, 43

MacIntyre, Alasdair, 33, 144–45
Malcolm, Norman, 5, 29–32, 44, 47–48
Martin, C.B., 150–52
Matson, Wallace, 145
Methodological conservatism, 92–108
Mill, John Stuart, 102
Miracles, 69–70
Mitchell, Basil, 112–13, 114–18

Naturalism, as alternative to theism, 131–40
Newman, John Henry, 76
Nielsen, Kai, 5, 182
Nonbelief
  attitude of believers toward, 108
  not an obstacle to judging the truth of religious claims, 22–24
  not merely withholding assent, 2–3

Paradigms, religious belief and, 116–27
Phillips, D.Z., 4, 5, 34–42, 44–49
Philosophy of religion, nature of, 1–6
Plantinga, Alvin, 50–51, 70–84
Plato, 37, 38
Prayer, petitionary, 34–37

Preller, Victor, 184

Religious experiences, 18–22, 60–64, 66–67, 138–40, Chapter 5
  and traditional religious beliefs, 171–77
  argument for God's existence from, 151–53, 171–72
  criteria for the veridicality of, 145–51
  of the "presence of God", 141–45
  William James on, 141–43
Religious beliefs
  and methodological conservatism, 92–108
  as acts rather than actions, 102–3
  as basic, 79–92
  as framework principles, 27–32
  core vs. outer belt, 175–77
  initial presumption in favor of, 2–4
  meaning of, 32ff
  nature of, 106–8
  nonbelievers' understanding of, 15ff
  reasonable/unreasonable distinction and, 25ff
Ross, James, 5

Scientific realism and religious belief, 163–68
Sellars, Wilfrid, 17, 59, 68, 165–68

Skepticism
  and methodological conservatism, 97–99
  and religious belief, 3, 8–9, 178–80
Sklar, L., 96–101
Swinburne, Richard, 5, 137–39, 147–49

Tillich, Paul, 140

Via eminentiae and *via remotionis*, 53–54

Whitehead, Alfred North, 140
Winch, Peter, 32–34
Wittgenstein, Ludwig
  on disagreements about religion, 15–24
  on the nature of religious beliefs, 25–29